THE FALL OF THE ANC

To all the thinking people in South Africa

THE FALL OF THE ANC

What Next?

Prince Mashele & Mzukisi Qobo

PICADOR AFRICA

First published in 2014 by Picador Africa
an imprint of Pan Macmillan South Africa
Private Bag x19
Northlands
Johannesburg
2116

www.panmacmillan.co.za

ISBN 978-1-77010-314-6
e-ISBN 978-1-77010-315-3

Editing by Alison Lowry
Proofreading by Wesley Thompson
Design and typesetting by Triple M Design, Johannesburg
Cover design by K4

Printed and bound by Ultra Litho (Pty) Ltd

CONTENTS

ABBREVIATIONS

Amcu	Association of Mineworkers and Construction Union
ANC	African National Congress
ANCWL	ANC Women's League
ANCYL	ANC Youth League
AsgiSA	Accelerated and Shared Growth Initiative for South Africa
Azapo	Azanian People's Organisation
BEE	Black Economic Empowerment
Comintern	Communist International
Cosatu	Congress of South African Trade Unions
CPSA	Communist Party of South Africa
CPSU	Communist Party of the Soviet Union
DBSA	Development Bank of Southern Africa
DRC	Democratic Republic of the Congo
EFF	Economic Freedom Fighters
Gear	Growth, Employment and Redistribution
IFP	Inkatha Freedom Party
Jipsa	Joint Initiative on Priority Skills Acquisition
LIH	Lembede Investment Holdings
MERG	Macro-economic Research Group
MK	Umkhonto we Sizwe
NDR	National Democratic Revolution

NEC	National Executive Committee
NEF	National Economic Forum
NP	National Party
NUM	National Union of Mineworkers
OAU	Organisation of African Unity
PAC	Pan Africanist Congress
RDP	Reconstruction and Development Programme
SABC	South African Broadcasting Corporation
SACP	South African Communist Party
SADTU	South African Democratic Teachers Union
SANNC	South African Native National Congress
SOPA	Socialist Party of Azania
TRC	Truth and Reconciliation Commission
UDF	United Democratic Front
VOC	Vereenigde Oostindische Compagnie

PREFACE

Predicting the future is impossible. Political and social developments are, by their very nature, fluid, and anyone who pretends to have divine insight into the future should be doubted. Given the audacity of the title of this book – *The Fall of the ANC* – we could very easily find ourselves accused of such pretensions, especially since the ANC is still in existence and its president, Jacob Zuma, believes it will rule until the return of Jesus Christ.

Yet we must look at the clues in the present conduct of our political leadership and also learn from history to derive some sense of what the future could look like. In this book we reflect on what we see as the vegetative state of the ANC. We interpret current events to discern trends that paint a picture of possibilities that might lie ahead. Our main observation is that the ANC is disintegrating. This may not be something obvious to everyone at the moment but, as we suggest herein, it will not be long before this does become plain.

The party which at one stage in history carried the mantle of emancipation is not the same as the one we see led by President Jacob Zuma today. Yet it would be unfair to suggest that the seeds of its collapse began with Zuma. It is simply that Zuma tilted the focus of the party heavily in the direction trodden by many other liberation movements on the African continent. His is the same sad story of liberation politicians who start out as revolutionaries but later become klepto-crats interested mainly in what appears to us to be looting the state. Such leaders push their countries into the abyss and bequeath ruined foundations to future generations.

Some readers may be surprised to discover a fairly elaborate history of South Africa in these pages when they were expecting a quick plunge into the contemporary state of affairs in the ANC. If we had made such a hasty jump, we would have deprived some readers of access to the historical continuum which explains why the ANC and South Africa are the way they are today. The existence of the ANC cannot be under-stood apart from the history of racial domination and economic dis-possession of black South Africans since the Dutch first settled on the shores of the Cape of Good Hope more than three centuries ago. Since the ANC did not emerge in a vacuum, the political circumstances which pre-dated and conditioned its emergence are examined early on in the book.

The principal reason why we embarked on writing this book was because we want to alert South Africans to the dangerous implications for social stability and long-term national prosperity of the ANC's col-lapse. Questioning the ANC's readiness to govern is not in any way casting doubt on the need for South Africa to move from apartheid to democracy. Any sane person will agree that freedom is an inalien-able human right. What South Africans must not do is allow the ANC to blackmail us simply because it was once a liberation movement. In Africa, liberation movements have a terrible record of governance.

After two decades since the ANC took over power, a moment of reflection is required to understand what has gone wrong with the promise of a better society, and why we seem to be experiencing rever-sal instead of building on the vision painstakingly laid by leaders such as Nelson Mandela. Beyond diagnosis and critical assessment of the ANC, we also paint what we believe are inspiring signs of a desirable future.

This book is a modest contribution to a debate about taking large steps from the past into the future. It is aimed at stimulating discussions about political prospects beyond the ANC, and to reignite our passion for democracy, including the critical necessity of holding those who govern to account. It is also intended as a prompt for action as change comes when ordinary people realise their agency voice and power. It is when we *believe* we are powerless that we really lose our power.

Many books have been written about the ANC before. The gap we seek to fill is the paucity of analysis: why are we here, and what do all these developments mean for now and the future? This book is not written narrowly for an academic audience; it is meant for general readers who are interested in South African politics – its past, present and future – as seen through the prism of critical reflection. The book is in part polemical, in part historical musings for contextualisation, and in part analytical.

In a sense, this book is a culmination of numerous discussions we have had with various opinion shapers, leaders and ordinary South Africans about the state of the country's politics and the direction the ruling party is taking. In many instances, the concerns about the state of leadership and governance – which are the two major themes that feature prominently throughout this book – revolve around the ethos and practices of the ANC in power. At the centre of our enquiry is whether, upon assuming power, the party was ready to govern or not. We point to some tell-tale signs and marshal substantiated arguments that the ANC was not ready to govern and that it continues to fiddle in the dark.

INTRODUCTION

L ike all liberation movements on the African continent and elsewhere, the African National Congress (ANC) did not fall like a thunderbolt from the sky, to come and disrupt a peaceful and perfect political environment. It was formed by African nationalists in response to a long history of colonialism and racism. In other words, the ANC cannot be understood if it is not located in its historical context.

For three and a half centuries, the native people of South Africa had languished under the yoke of racism by successive white minority regimes. This was part of a larger European project which placed all human beings on Earth under the political and economic control of the Occident. The Dutch, who first settled in South Africa in 1652, were part of this project. When the British took over the Cape Colony in 1795, they, too, sought to strengthen their empire by annexing more territories in their mega, global imperialist scheme.

In the context of this global order, indigenous people all over the world were viewed by whites as objects that were ready and available to be used in furtherance of the interests of the master race, whites. They were an accessory to the process of capital accumulation, which essentially entailed the under-development of Africa for the purpose of modernising the metropolis in Europe. This was also the logic globally of the process of slavery. The evolution of racism in South Africa cannot be understood properly if it is not placed in its global context. In other words, racism is not a uniquely South African phenomenon, except in the ways in which it manifested itself in this country, but very much an extension of the global hierarchy of power, largely between the West and the non-Western parts of the world. When Malay, Indian and Chinese people were shipped in to toil in the vineyards, sugar plantations and mines of South Africa, the fundamental humanity of these people was regarded by their white masters as just as worthless as that of Africans.

Colonialism was not just a sadistic project in which whites simply sought to derive psychological gratification from the suffering of people of other races. It was, at its core, an economic project, a money-making affair. This is very much reflected in Cecil John Rhodes' dual enterprises of seeking to amass wealth through diamond and gold mining as well as paying homage to the British Empire by constructing a railway line from Cape to Cairo. When Europeans ventured in all directions out of their home continent, they did so in search of material resources which lay outside their continent. The political subjugation of natives of other continents and territories was meant to facilitate easy resource accumulation by Europeans. Notions of racial superiority served as a powerful psychological tool to assuage the all-too-human feeling of meting out pain to another human for selfish ends.

Colonialism and apartheid in South Africa were part of this European accumulation process. The diamonds, gold and other natural resources of the country were monopolised by European settlers, for their benefit locally and for the enjoyment of their folk back in Europe. In the process, the natives of this country were marginalised politically and used as tools in the bigger European accumulation project.

The marginalisation of natives in South Africa could not be secured without their total economic disempowerment. This meant that the natives had to be deprived of their means of livelihood in order for them to be transformed from their conditions of self-sufficiency into purchasable and exploitable labour. This was done systematically throughout the unfolding of the settlement schemes of successive Europeans in South Africa, and a raft of laws that followed, from placing limits on the locations in which natives could live to the extent to which they could accumulate wealth. Self-sufficiency had to be severely constrained in order to create a deep sense amongst the natives of dependence. Accordingly, at a time of politically induced material need they would look to the white man as a father and a benefactor of all that was good.

The formation of the Union government in 1910 marked a major turning point in the history of South Africa. Not only did it consolidate the joint accumulation interests of the English and Afrikaners but, more importantly, it thwarted the hopes of Africans in their quest for political freedom and economic emancipation. It was clear from the beginning that the Union of South Africa was to be presided over exclusively by whites. Africans were not to be part of the grand white deal. Given the fact that the Afrikaners had known a deep sense of injustice and had been subjected to the most humiliating and vile conditions by the British during the Anglo-Boer War, it is puzzling that they did not side with the marginalised natives, and that their sense of justice would not have awakened indignation at the oppression of the natives. Yet they went to bed with the English with whom they shared similar pigmentation.

What 1910 failed to achieve, however, was the total silencing of Africans. Ironically, the grand white deal served only to goad Africans into more organised forms of resistance. The formation of the ANC in 1912 was a direct response to the whites-only Union government. From the beginning, the ANC positioned itself as a nationalist formation that sought to break tribal walls and unite all Africans behind a common political agenda. This is what we mean when we say the ANC did not fall like a thunderbolt from the sky, to come and disrupt a peaceful and perfect political environment. It was formed as a response to a long history of colonialism and apartheid. Its struggles were born of the felt reality and pain suffered by black people under the reign of an exclusively white political elite.

Viewed from this standpoint, the ANC was indeed a historic necessity with a compelling moral claim. As we point out in this book, African nationalism was a response to racism. The transition from apartheid to democracy in 1994 marked a major milestone in the aspirations of Africans. Essentially, 1994 represented a political victory for the ANC, and created great expectations of better governance and economic emancipation for the historically disempowered black majority. These expectations were not without justification, for the ANC had for decades projected itself as the opposite of apartheid. Inhumanity lay at the core of apartheid. It was no mistake that after its vicious expression by the Afrikaner Nationalist government since 1948 – continuing where the Union government and British rule before it left off – apartheid was officially condemned as a crime against humanity by the United Nations on 30 November 1973.

The ANC aimed to restore the basic humanity of all South Africans – black and white – and to redefine the terms of race relations in South Africa. This was a noble cause and it was to earn the ANC legitimacy in the eyes of many. It allowed the ANC to deepen its roots in the psyche of many black people in South Africa. As a fighting movement the ANC could not be described in any way other than valiant, even though it committed excesses in the trenches of the struggle. This, however, was not indicative of how the ANC would fare when it took power.

Fighting for the liberation of the oppressed is one thing; governing a nation with as complex a history and the social challenges that South Africa has today is quite another. Having spent almost five decades as a protest movement, and three more decades as an underground organisation, the ANC had accumulated experience as a liberation movement, not in governing a country. It had perfected its tactics and strategies as a liberation movement. Its preoccupation was fighting the

4

gigantic monster of apartheid, but as a disempowered political vehicle. It had to succour itself on myths and dream up better ways of convincing black people of the glorious possibilities to be brought about by liberation. It was trained in fighting, in being fluent in rhetoric, and in being able to identify enemies and eliminate them quickly.

Being an underground and exiled organisation, ducking and diving enemy forces, did not afford the ANC the time or the luxury of exploring detailed ideas about the form and institutions of a future government in South Africa. It lacked the capacity properly to envision, beyond the wish list of the Freedom Charter, what a functional political, social and economic system might look like when apartheid ended. Its dreams were big but its resources were meagre. A political struggle such as the one waged by the ANC was, in the main, a survivalist struggle. What was paramount and urgent under such conditions was to ensure the survival of militants and activists in order to sustain the struggle. Imagining the details of a future government must have been seen as the luxury of those who already operated under conditions of liberty.

It is understandable, therefore, that, apart from the Freedom Charter which was adopted in 1955, the ANC did not have any other blueprint for governing before it was unbanned in 1990. In other words, before it was unbanned, the party's focus was elsewhere – on keeping the organisation and its core objectives, namely, bringing an end to apartheid in South Africa and the liberation of black people in that country, alive in exile. In the heat of the liberation struggle, the idea of developing plans for a future government would have been idealism. And producing a detailed plan as proof that it had a clear idea as to what it would do if it were to seize power was not done.

Two years after it was unbanned, in 1992 the ANC declared itself ready to govern. It was clear from the political events of the time that the party was the presumed government-in-waiting. What was not clear, though, was whether the ANC was indeed ready to govern. This was taken for granted. As the party had not been in government before, there were doubts expressed from many quarters and questions were asked about what the ANC would do as soon as it ascended to power – hence its haste to issue policy guidelines to assure the world that there was no need to panic.

But, as we argue in this book, the reality was that the ANC was *not* ready to govern. It was an imperfect party. Then two significant things happened and the ANC found itself at a crossroads: the ANC's ideological and financial sponsor, Soviet Russia, crumbled to its knees as a result of internal economic implosion; and simultaneously, the last apartheid president, F.W. de Klerk, started to initiate political reforms. A confluence of events brought enormous pressure on the ANC to consider seriously the option of negotiating power-sharing and to be at the coalface of designing a new constitutional arrangement for a democratic South Africa. None of this was part of the ANC's original script, which had toyed with notions of 'insurrectionary seizure' of power, which was to suggest armed revolt launched by the ANC's military wing Umkhonto we Sizwe (MK). This was a view deeply entrenched amongst a thinking segment of the ANC's leadership, and most of whom were also part of the high-command structures of the South African Communist Party (SACP). A great deal of what the party thought it would achieve was informed by an inflated sense of self and by sheer naivety.

Such innocence was to be expressed again in respect of the ANC's over-estimation of its capacity to lead large-scale change in the social and economic structure upon taking power. Many in the party thought that the state had the capacity to deliver a whole range of basic needs to the poor black majority; to transfer the commanding heights of the economy to the state; and to create vast swathes of businesses run by black people. This naive thinking found expression in the long list of services the new ANC government promised to deliver through the party's Reconstruction and Development Programme (RDP). Within two years, however, the newly elected ANC government realised that it could not deliver the manna it promised from its imagined heaven.

Access to state information made the ANC realise that, political aspirations notwithstanding, the state did not have the financial where-withal to pay for RDP promises. This is why the Growth, Employment and Redistribution (Gear) programme was adopted in 1996, regard-less of ideological protests by ideologically over-zealous members of the tripartite alliance who, in any case, failed to produce credible eco-nomic policy frameworks which could be usable templates for govern-ing a country. They were still slumbering in the dreams and idealism of Soviet-era communist activism.

The introduction of Gear represented a clear ideological U-turn: from a 'redistribution-first' enthusiasm to a 'growth-first' realistic approach. While in exile, the ANC had not entertained this debate. The debate arose when the party was already in government, a sign that the ANC had not anticipated the complexities it encountered once it was in gov-ernment. It is one thing to expect, and quite another to experience. This is what experience taught the ANC in its early days in government.

The unpreparedness of the ANC to deal with the complexities of gov-erning and to deliver on socio-economic promises was not immediate-ly realised by the masses of expectant poor people and other observers. The moral stature of the ANC was so overwhelming that there was lit-tle space for critical reflection. All the propaganda of apartheid that projected the ANC as a terrorist organisation, led by savages who were ready to kill, was proven wrong.

A great deal happened during the transition that could have led this country into a civil war. The Bisho and Boipatong massacres, 'black-on-black' violence involving members of the Inkatha Freedom Party (IFP) and the ANC, the killing of Chris Hani – all could easily have ignited South Africa into a racial and tribal inferno. But the ANC prevailed; it led the majority of black people away from the bloodbath, paving the way for a relatively peaceful transition from apartheid to democracy.

The development of a new Constitution served to reassure South Africans that the country was on a path to a better future. The fact that the Constitution combined political and socio-economic rights was an inspiration to those who had been oppressed politically and economically. It also provided crucial guarantees to white South Africans who had been made to believe the *swart gevaar* (black peril) racist propaganda. The future appeared bright for both black and white South Africans.

The spirit of inclusiveness demonstrated by the ANC during the transition years was reassuring. That the ANC and the National Party (NP) agreed to serve in a government of national unity created a sense of hope that it was possible for blacks and whites to work together in building a new country, different from the segregationist politics of the apartheid government. This was an important example for ordinary South Africans to emulate. It served to relax racial attitudes and to make citizens see hope in the future. As such, the post-apartheid order was comparably, and vastly, better normatively than the apartheid regime, although it was not quite the ideal system envisioned by the progenitors of the new South Africa.

The magnanimity of Nelson Mandela as the first president of democratic South Africa was a decisive factor in holding the fragile South African nation together. Imperfect as it was, the Truth and Reconciliation Commission (TRC) made a symbolic contribution to national healing. While families that had lost relatives found it difficult to cope with the gory details of what had happened to their loved ones, the profoundly cathartic drama of Archbishop Desmond Tutu breaking down in tears and white people asking for forgiveness went a mile in reducing the intensity of our national trauma. This was both a moment of perplexity and great optimism, marked by intense emotion about what we had managed to achieve as a nation, given our racial past.

All these factors contributed to building the confidence of South

Africans. If we could go through such a difficult period, surely the future would be better. Given the leadership role of the ANC in nursing the fragile transition, the party further gained the confidence of the country's citizens, both black and white. The party fast became a trusted guarantor of a better South Africa, embodying the aspirations of the previously oppressed majority, and reassuring doubting citizens among whites.

Difficulties notwithstanding, the political transition into democracy was fairly well managed. It is thus not surprising that a great deal of expectations arose about the future. In the hold-your-breath climate of the transition, suggesting that the ANC would not deliver on some of the promises it made in the RDP would have appeared like cynicism of the worst order. Back then, the promise of jobs and equality appeared like a dream waiting to happen. But time has now revealed that the early enthusiasm of the transition period was not wholly realistic. At best, as we suggest in the book, it was a false optimism. The promised economic fruits are yet to come. Very few people still enthuse about the 'rainbow nation'.

The moral stature of the ANC of Mandela lulled us into believing that the ANC would never succumb to the viruses of politics: of corruption, factionalism, moral decay and a general state of decline. The image of Mandela made his party appear like a club of monks, whose lives were only about sacrifice and nothing else; and whose faith was too strong to be broken by the power of the flesh. The gallantry of an organisation which had survived 30 years of a demanding underground liberation struggle placed a halo of heroism around the ANC.

It is easy to be a monk if you live in a monastery. The real test of a monk is not when he is in a monastery, but when he is facing battles and dealing with the many tribulations of the real world, and when encountering those who are not so saintly. Out there in the world, there are real temptations. We can only tell if a monk is able to resist the seductive power of beautiful women if he lives among them in the real world, not when the monk is restricted to the life of day and night prayers in the monastery.

Similarly, the real character of the ANC could not be discovered until the party gained and became entrenched in power. Its saintly pretensions could only be tested once its cadres occupied offices in government, and when they were entrusted with the authority to preside over the distribution of tenders and the power to use public funds. The aphorism of the British historian Lord Acton is well known: 'All power tends to corrupt; absolute power corrupts absolutely'. And, as we argue in this book, the ANC has in our view been corrupted beyond repair by the seductions of power.

As soon as ANC cadres in government discovered what they could do with public offices, they proved Lord Acton right. Soon, there was a big arms deal scandal that, as we argue in this book, implicated the party (collectively) and some of its cadres (individually) in corruption. The party and its cadres now knew that it was materially rewarding, and indeed very profitable, to hold an office in government. Corruption scandals involving ANC leaders are too many to enumerate and have been extensively covered in the media and other popular books. The party itself has been engaged brazenly in numerous capitalist investment schemes through its less-than-angelic investment company called Chancellor House.

While factionalism had historically been part of the ANC, the full extent of its destructiveness became more pronounced when the party was entrenched in power. In fact, the party now appears like a mega-patronage network, handsomely rewarding those who are on the right side of the party's factional divide. The fear of a loss of power in national or provincial government is not so much about the derailment of the National Democratic Revolution as it is about the loss of powerful levers to seemingly churn out patronage and pocket kick-backs from massive state contracts. Currently, the party is led by a president who himself was accused of corruption and who worked hard to quash any possibility of appearing before a court of law to answer to his charges (which were eventually withdrawn). Unlike his predecessors, Jacob Zuma is an endured president, not a respected leader.

Zuma's image has diminished with that of his party. To be a member of the ANC today means that you hold a ticket to a job in government, or, it seems to us, to a lucrative tender in the state and its ANC cadre-run companies. All manner of shady characters have joined the ANC. Unlike the sea, the party has no self-cleansing mechanism. The only thing that is left of the ANC is its glorious history. The problem is that it is increasingly becoming difficult for the ANC's history to be protected from the political immorality of the scoundrels who have inherited the history. Instead of inspiring hope, the ANC now induces fear about the future.

When we say the 'Fall of the ANC' in the title of the book, we do not mean it literally, nor do we mean the party's imminent death. We mean it in the sense of the party having become a pale shadow of its former self. It is as good as dead. Like parts of the skin that have become deadened and are lacking vitality, the ANC is denuded of ideological content, of a clear set of ideas about where to take the country into the future, and of a credible leadership that is fit for such a purpose. The notion that we present in this book of the fall of the ANC is in no way to be read as suggesting that the ANC will lose the elections in 2014, but rather that having lost relevance it is slowly but surely on its way out of power. It is also dead in the sense that it is a party of the past rather than a party which bears hopes of the future. There will probably be a building called Luthuli House, a National Executive Committee of the ANC, and its associated provincial and branch structures, but all these represent nothing substantive other than to repeat the mantra of slogans and momentarily celebrate the glory of past leaders and struggles.

Due to cut-throat factionalism and rampant corruption, the image of a glorious party, the moralistic party of Mandela, is gone – forever. The die is cast. It is an illusion to hope that the ANC can be rescued and restored to its former glory. What remains is a mega-patronage network, deployed to ensure that the party keeps its factions happy and that they work for it to win elections. There is never enough to feed everyone from the trove of the state, and therefore some will inevitably cross over to competing factions or start new political parties, the effect of which will be further to reduce confidence in the ANC. Outside of the ANC, discontent will continue to swell until ordinary people eventually see that the ANC has become an empty shell and is now only a nest that, we argue, breeds corruption. It is only a matter of time before South Africans realise that they have it within their power to boot this gang out of power. When this finally happens, the question will be: what next? The last part of this book deals with this very question.

Perhaps our naivety about the ANC's monkish pretensions could have been moderated. Had we looked around, the African continent could have taught us important lessons. If we had cared to seek knowledge from the experiences of Africans elsewhere, we would never have entertained the illusory idea of South African exceptionalism – that, for some inexplicable reason, the ANC would not behave like other liberation movements that have misgoverned African countries before.

From Ghana to Kenya, from Egypt to Zimbabwe, other Africans had already discovered the gap between promises and the actual behaviour of liberation movements after liberation movements have assumed power.[1] The potential of African revolutions to eat their own children had already been witnessed in such countries as Zaire, now the Democratic Republic of the Congo (DRC), under Mobutu Sese Seko. Kwame Nkrumah had already proven that a liberation hero can easily turn into a political villain. Indeed, the wave of post-colonial African politics had played itself out, in a way that revealed the inner deceptiveness of the great African promise.

Yet South Africans continued to believe the ANC propaganda of selfless revolutionary cadres, committed to the 'National Democratic Revolution' and the economic emancipation of the masses of their people. As these promises were being made, it was becoming increasingly obvious that the cadres were getting richer and that the material gap between them and their masses was yawning. The new parties which will emerge from what we contend is the corrupt womb of the ANC will still carry its seed and prey upon the gullibility and hero-worshipping of the masses. They will promise to construct a paradise on Earth at the twinkle of an eye. It has happened before elsewhere on the African continent, as this book points out, and it will happen again. All South Africans needed to do was learn lessons from history.

South Africa under the ANC has moved from a promising beginning to now manifesting signs of disaster. This has led observers to speculate about whether there is potential for the party ever to lose power. This question does not arise simply because those who entertain it dislike the ANC. It is necessitated by the reality of a dominant party being prone to political arrogance. An environment where a party is always assured of victory is invariably accompanied by a tendency towards lesser accountability in the political system. This is precisely what has given rise to concerns regarding the continued dominance of the ANC. The sooner the party is confined to the grave the better for South Africa.

Given the position of power that the ANC currently enjoys, it shouldn't be surprising to us that the party would be emboldened to believe that it will rule South Africa until Jesus Christ returns, as its president has boasted repeatedly. Power makes its wielders believe they are historically destined to preside over societies. At the height of their power, few rulers can anticipate their fall. Given its heroic history of struggle, the ANC may believe that South Africans will remain forever grateful to the party, and thus reward the party with eternal power.

The Greek philosopher Heraclitus said that change is constant. Like other societies, ours too will evolve. Even on grand scales, civilisations and cultures get overtaken by others. Political systems evolve, and human beings are not the mirror image of their forebears a hundred years ago in an identical social structure. Old citizens will eventually die, children will grow up. And when children grow up, they will not do everything their parents taught them to do. They will choose their own style of dress, their own food, their own hobbies and, indeed, their own politics.

A parent who claims to know the destiny of his child is a dreamer – nothing more. Similarly, ANC members who claim to know that South Africa will be governed by the party until Christ returns are either fantastic dreamers or else they are groping in the dark. They simply do not have a clue. It is not speculative divination that matters, but analysis. Analysis can help us in the exploration of possibilities on the basis of identifiable social conditions and analysis will enable us to identify and examine various possible scenarios.

The scenarios we offer here are based on specific social conditions that are logically imaginable. There are things we know, and there are things we do not know. The things we know can assist us to make projections into the future. The things we do not know make us moderate our prophetic pretensions. No one knows the future. The future can only be seen through imagination, assisted by rigorous analysis, and imagination can be wholly wrong, especially if it is not based on prevailing conditions. If it is based on the analysis of current conditions, and if it does not suppress the possibilities that logically arise from particular sets of circumstances, imagination can sometimes be right.

On the basis of the current state of politics in South Africa – of corruption, factionalism, the use of politics as a means of accumulation, all of which have become emblematic of the ANC – we have come to the conclusion that if the party does not make a serious U-turn, it will ruin itself and our country at the same time. We are pessimistic about the prospects of the ANC undergoing a Damascus conversion that would reset its character and behaviour in a way that connects positively with the core dreams and aspirations of South Africans. The ANC is incorrigible. Its leaders have chosen to suspend all rationality and have instead delegated thinking to the stomach.

Our confidence in future change should thus not lie with the ANC reforming itself, but in the rational capacity of human beings. There is no one particular party we believe is the bearer of such change. The agency power of ordinary citizens participating both in political processes and in civil society is where we see the ability to bring about change.

If the ANC were to further ruin itself and South Africa, what would ensue would depend on the readiness of current opposition parties to take advantage of the new circumstances. We highlight in this book some of the things that the Democratic Alliance (DA) or some other new party would need to do in preparation for the future. We point out the strengths and weaknesses of various parties. From the outset, we plead guilty to the charge of analytical ruthlessness. We do not in any way present ourselves as objective – whatever objective means. It would be fanciful to be objective when the political situation in the country points in the direction of the abyss.

Politics in a democracy is a game of constant readjustments. A party which does not readjust itself constantly to align with ever-evolving social dynamics eventually dies. So far, there is little evidence to suggest that the ANC is doing this, which is why we think the party is headed for a terrible crash. The timing of this we do not know, and we do not want to pretend to hold a crystal ball. We leave that to diviners. We also cannot tell if any of the current political parties will ever take over power, for they all have weaknesses that need to be addressed before they could be viewed by voters as genuine alternatives. One thing we should be conscious of, as the French historian Alexis de Tocqueville reminds us, is that major revolutionary events can be unpredictable even by astute observers, despite the fact that signs may be painted on the horizon.[2]

As to the ideal, we know that it cannot and shall never be attained by people who sit and wait for change to impose itself. It is ordinary men and women who make change happen through their conscious actions. The outcome may effect a seismic shift in the social structure, but such change does not always take the form of a Big Bang. Rather it comes about as a result of the incremental and cumulative efforts of individuals. Unlike in the jungle, human societies are not adjusted automatically by nature. As human beings, we have been endowed with a special gift: consciousness. We can choose what we want to do, and what we do not want to do. The choices we make determine the nature of our societies.

The German philosopher and political theorist Herbert Marcuse was correct in observing:

> An immediate unity of reason and reality never exists. The unity comes after a lengthy process, which begins at the lowest level of nature and reaches up to the highest form of existence, that of a free and rational subject, living and acting in the self-consciousness of its potentialities.[3]

Indeed, it is not nature that produces an ideal state in society. It is the conscious actions of humankind that eventually alter a social environment where there is no unity between reason (human ideals) and reality (nature as it confronts humankind). The process of constructing unity is one that proceeds from a lower state to a higher stage. When individuals make a personal choice, and when individuals act upon their choices, that process will alter the less ideal circumstances of individuals, thereby facilitating a move to an ideal situation, created by the conscious actions of individuals themselves.

As with social structures, in politics reality does not get adjusted automatically by some natural process either. Individuals, acting consciously as free and rational subjects, determine the course of politics. The idea that only a mass of people can change society, a mass acting as if it is operated by some force beyond the power of the individual, is a fallacy. There is no society without an individual, but there can be an individual without society. In a free society, an individual chooses which church, which soccer team or which political party to join. It is true that these societies can target an individual, but the individual can refuse to join. And, if it is a democracy, there is nothing associations can do to force an individual to join them. So, who said individuals cannot change their environment if they act consciously as free and rational subjects? This book envisions a range of possibilities.

Chapter 1

A HISTORIC NECESSITY

The arrival and settlement of white people in South Africa set in motion the process of constructing a defective society. Very little can be understood without considering the chain of history that has produced what we see in contemporary South Africa. The country today is a culmination of what white people have been doing since the arrival of Jan van Riebeeck in 1652. The whites who worked to shape South Africa had links with countries in Europe. From the outset, the hand of Europe's political economy was active in moulding this southern tip of Africa. In the broader scheme of things, these links were part of a bigger project: to make the whole world minister to the needs of Europeans. The famous British economist John Maynard Keynes captured the essence of this grand project appositely:

What an extraordinary episode in the economic progress of man that age was which came to an end in August, 1914 ... The inhabitant of London could order by telephone, sipping his morning tea in bed, the various products of the whole Earth, in such quantity as he might see fit, and reasonably expect their delivery upon his doorstep ... He could secure forthwith, if he wished it, cheap and comfortable means of transit to any country or climate without passport or

other formality ... and could then proceed abroad to foreign quarters,
without knowledge of their religion, language, or such customs ....[1]

When the Vereenigde Oostindische Compagnie (VOC) – otherwise known as the Dutch East India Company – first settled in the Cape of Good Hope in the mid-seventeenth century, the grand plan was not to initiate economic development in South Africa. The motive was to use the Cape as a refreshment station servicing Dutch ships as they sailed to and from India and other territories of the East. This was to ensure that Europeans gained access to resources from other parts of the world. It was for this reason that, from 1652 to 1795, the Dutch did not move into the interior of South Africa to construct roads or put in place other infrastructures associated with the development of a modern economy. This was not part of their politico-economic scheme. In their estimation, there was little value in the interior of South Africa. What mattered at the time was the Eastern sea route. As Roger Southall, a South African sociologist, observes: 'Settler colonialism in southern Africa was born out of an accident in that the origins of white settlement at the tip of the continent were the product of the ambition of Dutch and British merchant capital to expand their trade with India, and their need for a supply depot at the Cape.'[2]

The poor Europeans who were brought into South Africa by the VOC were generally left to their own devices or to fend for themselves in the new and foreign environment – with little assistance from the company. Thus the early, wandering Afrikaners got into conflict with the Khoisan, the indigenous people of the Cape. To survive, the Afrikaners were compelled by circumstances to thieve livestock and plunder the land owned by the indigenous population. In a way, this resembled Thomas Hobbes's state of nature, except that it was not a war 'of every man, against every man'[3] – it was a war of newcomers against those who had settled first.

Jan van Riebeeck understood the workings of the law of the jungle perfectly. He recorded in his journal that indigenous people 'had to be told that they had now lost [their] land as a result of war and had no alternative but to admit that [the land] was no longer theirs'.[4] There was no room for negotiation. The indigenous people of the Cape were forced to succumb to the despotism of the gun. The principle of first occupancy was disregarded ruthlessly. The new lords had arrived. Everything had to give way to the wants and voracity of the newcomers from Europe. From these early beginnings, it was to be expected that South Africa would become a country characterised by racial tensions. The economic and social foundations were faulty, and bound to culminate in a defective society. Race framed social reality henceforth.

The British wrested the Cape from the Dutch in 1795, but they did not come as messiahs to save South Africa or to develop black people. That was the last thing on their minds. At the time, Great Britain was a leading participant in wars of conquest among European empires. The barrel of a gun was a means through which to enforce the expropriation of vast territories of land with no regard for the sanctity of human life. It was a barbaric civilisation. Back then, as is still the case now, the route to the East was strategic, both for commercial and military purposes. Major European powers had for a long time kept this route in their sights. Great Britain thus came to South Africa to kick out the militarily weak Holland in order to control that lucrative sailing route. Indeed, the mighty British Empire had formed its East India Company in 1600, two years before the Dutch formed their Dutch East India Company. In Europe, Holland was an ant compared to the elephantine Britain, which is why the Dutch had to beat a hasty retreat as soon as they witnessed the signs that the mighty British Empire was set on annexing the Cape of Good Hope. Britain's intentions were consummated by the proclamation of British sovereignty over the entire Cape at a ceremony the Dutch painfully witnessed, after which the flag of Saint George was hoisted to signal the footprints of the British Empire.[5]

Upon arrival in the Cape, the British were quick to redefine power relations. In order to grow the English population in the region, Great Britain had to import her surplus population to South Africa. This was bound to aggravate the already tense relations between white settlers and the indigenous African population. More land had to be found to settle Britain's imported population. The nine Frontier Wars (fought between 1779 and 1879) were essentially about the making of space for white – mainly English – settlers by removing Africans forcibly from their land. Resistance by Africans was suppressed by the barrel of the gun. In 1811, the then governor of the Cape, Sir John Cradock, reported back to London about the success of his land-grabbing mission:

> *I am happy to add that in the course of this service there has not shed more Kaffir blood than would be necessary to impress on the minds of these savages a proper degree of terror and respect.*[6]

This is how Africans were described in British officialdom – 'Kaffirs' and 'savages', whose worthless blood could be shed whenever some British plenipotentiary felt like it. British imperialists had their own ideas of what was the necessary quantity of Kaffir blood to be shed, and what was a proper degree of terror to be visited upon Africans. Placed in context, this attitude towards Africans was part of a racially defined global political order – or shall we say, disorder? – that placed the Occident above the whole of the human race. White people all over the world believed themselves to be at the top of the hierarchy of race, a belief, some might argue, which still persists to this day. In Africa, this attitude found concrete expression through slave trade and colonialism. People other than whites were regarded as objects that could be sold or exchanged for the fulfilment of whites' interests.

As the new colonial masters of the Cape Colony, the British did not only disrupt the lives of Africans. They also made life extremely difficult for the Afrikaners who had been living in the Cape. The abolition of slavery in 1834 meant that Afrikaners had to relearn how to live without relying on slave labour. This was the main trigger that set off the Great Trek in 1835. The Afrikaner leader Piet Retief, one of the first Voortrekkers, expressed the Afrikaners' core grievance poignantly: 'We complain of the several losses, which we have been forced to sustain by the emancipation of our slaves, and the vexatious laws, which have been enacted respecting them.'[7] The Afrikaners harboured the hope that life would be better outside the British-controlled Cape Colony. They thus packed their wagons and left, drifting northwards into South Africa's interior.

Since the Great Trek, numerous conflicts have taken place in the making of South Africa – between the Afrikaners and Africans, between the English and Afrikaners, and between the English and Africans. Almost all the major conflicts were about land. If they refused to give up the land they occupied, the Africans were attacked either by the British or by the Afrikaners. The authority of African kings and chiefs was undermined and disrupted by white settlers on the basis of the whims of the settler. The Afrikaners were attacked by the English if they stood in the way of Britain's strategic interests. In 1843, for example, the Voortrekkers were kicked out of Port Natal by the English, where they had settled following their Great Trek from the Cape.[8]

Located along the east coast, the British viewed Port Natal as part of the strategic route to India and the Far East. They would not tolerate that part of South Africa being controlled by people who harboured strong grievances against Great Britain. The Voortrekkers had to be sent packing. They then drifted further north into the interior, and in 1860 declared themselves the rulers of the South African Republic in territory north of the Vaal River. This was the build-up to the creation of the two Afrikaner-controlled so-called republics: the Orange Free State and the Transvaal. This did not bother the British much, because the land-locked northern parts of South Africa were at the time not considered strategic. But this was not to last long.

The discovery of diamonds in Griqualand in 1867, and gold on the

Witwatersrand in 1886, transformed South Africa in ways never imagined before. During this giddy era which drew all manner of people to
the continent from various parts of Europe, the country became part
of a global supply chain that fed Europe's hunger for precious metals.
Resource hunger is not something that was an invention of the Chinese
in the twenty-first century as Western commentary would sometimes have us believe. Westerners had been at it for a very long time.
Europeans and people from North America descended upon South
Africa in search of fortunes. Individuals such as Cecil John Rhodes,
Charles Dunell Rudd, Alfred Beit, Barney Barnato, Leander Starr
Jameson – the first generation of Randlords – were among famous
European fortune hunters who used South Africa's mineral wealth to
immortalise their names; names that are today synonymous with the
development of South Africa's mining industry. Africans were marginalised and denied meaningful economic participation. They were used
mainly as cheap labour. Various laws and regulations were enacted to
prevent them from trading in precious metals.

The development of a nationwide economic system in South Africa
was fuelled by the discovery of diamonds and gold. Before then, successive white settlers were interested mainly in managing the affairs of
the Cape of Good Hope – either as a refreshment station, as in the case
of Holland, or as both a refreshment station and a militarily strategic
naval post, as in the case of the British. The movement of settlers into
the interior was motivated by the need for settlement land and sub-
sistence purposes. Even the farm-loving Afrikaners were at the time
not commercial farmers. In the main, they were farming to fill their
stomachs.

The fact that South Africa did not have a developed road and railway
infrastructure made it almost impossible for Afrikaner farmers to be
part of the global agricultural export system, besides which agro-pro-
cessing was under-developed at the time. There was no processed food-
stuff to export out of South Africa. The fact that, since 1795, the Cape

Colony (and virtually the rest of South Africa) had been a British colony also made it difficult for Afrikaners to establish channels of trade with the outside world. Great Britain would never allow this to happen, as they would not want Afrikaner farmers to pose a commercial threat to farmers back in Britain. It should be noted that this period was the heyday of mercantilism. Besides, the Afrikaners were themselves very poor and were not in any position to engage in any large-scale trade. They were roaming the land for survival. As the historian C.W. de Kiewiet captures it: 'Though they never became true nomads, the mark of nomadism was upon them, and their dominant traits were those of restless and narrow existence.'[9]

The discovery of diamonds and gold awakened Great Britain to the economic potential of South Africa and the country began to be viewed as an important source of valuable mineral resources. It was no longer merely the country whose position made it a strategic sea-way to the East. The interior was no longer viewed as a useless patch of land, left to roaming, survivalist Afrikaners or despised African 'tribesmen'. As the global centre of the diamond trade, London now looked to South Africa for much-needed supplies and soon, too, the vaults of the Bank of England began to brim with South African gold, buttressing the gold standard in Europe and North America.

These new developments served to increase the politico-economic capital of South Africa among the political powers that dominated the world at the time. Instead of leaving the country to the whims of some adventure-obsessed British governor or to roaming Afrikaners, Great Britain was now prepared to spend money and to sacrifice her soldiers to fight wars in South Africa. Any action by the Afrikaners in 'their' two republics that threatened British economic interests was met with the real threat of war. Aware of this, British representatives and nobility in South Africa adopted a provocative and jingoistic attitude towards African leaders and the Afrikaners. The belligerent attitude of Alfred Milner and Cecil John Rhodes in the events leading to the Anglo-Boer

War is a perfect example. These two warmongers were prepared to ride roughshod over anyone standing in the way of British economic interests. Milner and Rhodes had no time for the attempts by Afrikaner leaders to avert war. The political and racial tensions arising from this period continue to define South Africa's social relations to this today. While they may not show it in the public domain, the English and the Afrikaners still harbour ill-feelings towards each other, in subtle ways that keep old fires of hatred burning.

The grand deal

After a long century of conflicts and wars, the English and Afrikaners realised the symbiotic value of co-governing South Africa. Following the Anglo-Boer War, they struck a political deal which led to the formation of the Union of South Africa in 1910. Jan Smuts, the brain behind the creation of the Union, was very clear regarding the position of Africans in this new political construct. As one biographer, Antony Lentin, points out: 'Smuts accepted as a fact of life the Boer refusal to recognise the black man as an equal.'[10] Smuts was perhaps the most intellectually respected Afrikaner of his time. Indeed, he remains one of the few revered South Africans of the twentieth century, trailing not far behind Nelson Mandela in international acclaim. And yet his educated mind failed to appreciate the simple biblical principle that all men are equal before God.

The white, grand deal of 1910 was based on the exclusion of the Africans from the governing of South Africa. Everything else that followed this deal was intended to safeguard the socio-economic interests of the white population, and to guarantee the role of South Africa as a supplier of natural resources and raw material to Europe and North America.

Since 1910, there have been numerous deals among white politicians.

They saw the emergence and disappearance of various political players, culminating in the ascendance of a virulent form of Afrikaner nationalism that captured state power in 1948. The National Party (NP) was unapologetic about the oppression of the Africans. Essentially, the introduction of apartheid was an expression of the crudity of a white supremacist ideology, the essence of which was the dehumanisation of the Africans.

Fundamentally, apartheid was a continuation of a long tradition of racism – from slavery to racial discrimination throughout the evolution of the mining industry in South Africa. There are those who would like to project Afrikaners in general as the most racist when compared to the English, as if racism was authored by the Afrikaners. It is true that Afrikaner nationalism was founded on racist supremacist beliefs and drew on national socialism which developed in Germany, but it also borrowed a great deal from the racism of the English.[11] In fact, the foundations of racial discrimination as an economic policy are found in the genesis and evolution of the mining industry, historically owned largely by the English. It is here that racial violence was laid bare in its social, political and economic expression.

When Cecil John Rhodes was dissatisfied with the performance of parliament in the Cape, he worked his way cleverly to become a parliamentarian himself. His main objective was eventually to use the then parliament to advance the interests of the mining industry. As a mining mogul already, Rhodes positioned himself as someone who could assist parliament with regard to matters pertaining to mining. This is how he was appointed chairperson of a parliamentary committee to explore measures to stem trade in illicit diamonds in 1882. Among other things, it was as a result of Rhodes's recommendations that parliament adopted the draconian Diamond Trade Act of 1882. The Act allowed the stripping naked of black mineworkers and the scouring of their hair, mouths and armpits for any possible theft of diamonds, measures that were not applied to white miners. It was also due to Rhodes's influence that government granted the mining industry powers to implement racist regulations in the mines. During this time:

> *Kimberley mine owners also gained government approval for a new system of searching that affected both black and white workers. All workers below the rank of manager were required to pass through search houses on entering the mines and leaving them. Separate search houses were set up for black and white workers. Blacks were ordered to strip naked and were subjected to degrading body searches. Whites did not have to take off their clothes and underwent only a limited visual inspection.*[12]

In the Cape Colony Rhodes sponsored the infamous law, the Masters and Servants Act, known as the 'Every Man Wallop his own Nigger Bill'. Here the roots of apartheid are laid bare. The idea that, in the workplace, black and white workers should be treated differently, which was at the heart of apartheid's economic system, was already being implemented 66 years before the apartheid government took office. The subjection of black people to indignity by whites was a system Cecil John Rhodes perfected long before the word 'apartheid' was even coined. Rhodes was not apologetic about it. He expressed his racist attitude confidently: 'As long as the natives remain in a state of barbarism we must treat them as a subject race and be lords over them.'[13] It was an objective that was to be enforced barbarically. The link between Rhodes's racist thinking and what the architects of apartheid implemented later on cannot be clearer.

Even the idea of separate reserves for blacks has its origins in race thinking long before apartheid was officially introduced. This idea is also traceable to Rhodes's pronouncements. This is what he said: 'Now I come to the question of Title. My idea is that the natives should be in Reserves and not mixed up with the white man.'[14] The claim that, historically, the English have a better track record than the Afrikaners

27

when it comes to their racial attitudes is propaganda, which cannot be supported by evidence. In fact, the only thing Afrikaners had to do was cut and paste from the ready-made work of the English. The Afrikaners had an easy job: refine the racially discriminatory inventions of the English, give the policy a name – apartheid – and spin a vast web of racially discriminatory laws that would criminalise even social acts such as inter-racial marriages or the use of amenities designated for one racial group. Apartheid placed a particular emphasis on ethnicity and race, and justified these on the basis of selective biblical texts in order to ground apartheid within a perverted version of Christian religion. Accordingly, Afrikaners regarded themselves as a people specially chosen by God, and their black counterparts as sub-human condemned by the Almighty to live a lowly life. Religious institutions, in particular the Dutch Reformed Church, would be deployed psychologically to achieve the ends of apartheid.

Even though Afrikaners and the English were embroiled in intermittent conflicts throughout the nineteenth century, they both were part of the white supremacist continuum constructed since 1652. The essence of this political continuum has been the marginalisation of the Africans, and the empowerment of whites. It does not matter whether these were English or Afrikaner whites: the subjugation of Africans has been at the centre of the white project in South Africa. Afrikaner academic Sampie Terreblanche exposes the core of this racist project aptly:

> *The colonial powers and white colonists [marginalised Africans] in mainly three ways: firstly, by creating political and economic power structures that put them in privileged and entrenched positions* vis-à-vis *the indigenous population groups; secondly, by depriving indigenous people of land, surface water, and cattle; and, thirdly, by reducing slaves and indigenous people to different forms of unfree and exploitative labour. These three threads have run ominously*

through South Africa's modern history, from the mid-seventeenth until the late twentieth century.[15]

The making of modern South Africa, therefore, cannot be understood outside the overarching framework of the grand deal that has under-pinned all the politico-economic schemes of successive white regimes since the first white settlers set foot on South African shores. The historic subjugation and impoverishment of Africans is one side of the coin. The other side is the systematic upliftment of whites from poverty. These two sides of the same coin are linked dialectically, and have no meaning if read independently of each other. In other words, the conditions of under-development of Africans cannot be understood outside the historical process that led to the economic empowerment of whites as a social group in South Africa. White wealth has a direct link to black poverty, and the reverse is equally true. Contemporary attempts to explain the two as if they have had no historical, causal relationship are mischievous.

The genesis of African nationalism

As white settlers were unfolding their grand schemes, Africans did not take this lying down. From the first Frontier War of 1779 to the last war of resistance (the Bambatha Rebellion of 1906), from King Moshoeshoe to King Sekhukhune, Africans engaged in different forms of resistance. The greatest weakness of the African attempts to resist colonialism was that African kings and chiefs were themselves not united, and the colonialists took advantage of this.

The birth of African nationalism would not be possible unless all Africans saw themselves as belonging to one nation. The fact that Africans were ruled by kings and chiefs who harboured narrow notions of identity was a major impediment to the development of a larger African identity. From time to time, African traditional leaders waged wars against each other. Amongst the most sustained of military campaigns by Africans against each other was in the period between 1813 and 1830, the Mfecane. In this period, King Shaka Zulu terrorised other Africans in the process of constructing and enlarging his Zulu kingdom. In today's South Africa, historians present divergent stories about the Mfecane, but although the narratives may be different, that Africans waged wars against each other cannot be disputed. Historical facts cannot be bent in the direction of those who wish to deploy history in the service of their current intentions.

The problem with history is that it is a narration by the living about the dead. It is impossible to raise Shaka or Mzilikazi from the grave to tell us what exactly they were up to when they attacked Moshoeshoe's people and other Africans. We are therefore at the mercy of all manner of reconstructionists who claim to be historians. History can also be the story of the history-maker. Human beings being what they are, even if it were possible for Shaka to rise from his tomb, nobody knows if he would tell the truth. People do lie about their real intentions. Very few people want posterity to view them in a bad light.

Whites have for centuries buttressed their political schemes with lies. Narratives of apartheid as 'separate development' abound, even as evidence proves that apartheid was about the development of whites and the under-development of blacks. Take the case of the notorious architect of apartheid, Hendrik Verwoerd, for example. He knew only too well that racial segregation was meant to keep Africans in inferior conditions, but he cooked the lie that segregation 'gives the native a chance to develop that which is his own and to develop pride and self-respect instead of being humiliated in an effort to mimic whites'.[16] Only those who are willingly gullible would buy this distorted story. The fact was that Verwoerd did not want blacks to dilute the purity of what he thought was a superior race – whites.

A good example, in our view, of a subtle reinterpretation of history to offer a benign image of apartheid is the account by the historian Hermann Giliomee in *The Last Afrikaner Leaders*, who offers that Verwoerd

> *introduced a system of mass public education for black and coloured pupils that emphasised primary education with a focus on the acquisition of basic skills. At that stage the labour market demanded unskilled and semi-skilled black labour rather than well-educated school leavers expecting white-collar jobs.*[17]

Here Verwoerd is repackaged and sold to us as a man of good intentions, who went the extra mile to educate black and coloured children. It is as if that's the best Verwoerd could have offered, nothing more. Another implication to Giliomee's revisionism is that blacks were destined by nature, and not social engineering, to occupy their lowly station and that Verwoerd had to simply accommodate them at that level, and therefore deserves a medal for doing so.

Accordingly, in Giliomee's version of the 'truth', Verwoerd played a messianic role towards black South Africans. It appears that, in Giliomee's interpretation, apartheid was not that bad; it was just an inconvenience that arose from a well-intentioned experiment that suffered minor glitches. Yet it is known that through the Bantu Education Act of 1953 Verwoerd unleashed a massive psychological onslaught on the black population and ensured that their station in life would be vastly different from that of the white community.

The very logic of apartheid, as Deborah Posel puts it, was

> *first and foremost the preservation of white racial political supremacy, as an essential requisite for perpetuating the supposed superiority of white 'civilisation' ... an attempt to sustain white political supremacy in ways that simultaneously promoted the cause of white economic prosperity.*[18]

Verwoerd declared his racist intentions quite plainly:

> *There is no place for the Bantu in the European community above the level of certain forms of labour ... What is the use of teaching the Bantu child mathematics when it cannot use it in practice? That is quite absurd. Education must train people in accordance with their opportunities in life, according to the sphere in which they live.*[19]

These cannot be the words of a philanthropist who sought genuinely to improve the conditions of black people, as the Giliomee hagiography implies. Verwoerd refers to 'the Bantu' as 'it'. Clearly he did not believe that black people were human beings. As far as he was concerned, human beings were only those who belonged to what he called 'the European community', from which blacks were excluded. No revisionist effort will alter this truth.

Giliomee's revisionism is also presented through concepts that seem to be meant to dupe unsuspecting readers. For example, his explanation that because 'the labour market demanded unskilled and semi-skilled black labour rather than well-educated school leavers' translates to Verwoerd's extension of poor-quality education to black and coloured children being a great act of philanthropy.

Giliomee's presentation of the so-called 'labour market' as if it was a thing decreed from above or fashioned by nature, unaffected by the dictates of apartheid laws, is also arguably misleading. The truth is that the labour market to which he refers was a social construct, made up of a web of firms owned by white people who were instructed by the apartheid government not to employ black people beyond specified levels. Arrangements such as the job colour bar were some of the mechanisms put in place to create an artificial labour market. Verwoerd had the power to instruct the firms owned by his white folk to employ black people in white-collar jobs, but he did not. Verwoerd was the political master of the 'labour market' to which Giliomee attributes the independent power to demand unskilled black labour.

It is precisely this racist thinking that gave rise to African national-ism. Having been excluded from the Union government in 1910, and having been denied political rights in the Union, Africans realised that they needed to put their differences aside and come together to con-front their common enemy. The year 1910 had marked the unity of the white race in South Africa. If Africans hoped to succeed in fighting for their rights, they, too, would have to unite, in the same way that white people had united in pursuit of their common purpose.

Ironically, it was the unity of the white race that encouraged the uni-ty of the black race. There is logic to this irony if we consider Isaac Newton's well-known third law of motion: 'When a first body exerts a force F_1 on a second body, the second body simultaneously exerts a force $F_2 = -F_1$ on the first body.' In the same way, when whites (F_1) came together to form the Union government in 1910, blacks (F_2) came together to form the African National Congress (then the South African Native National Congress) in 1912. The exclusion of blacks hav-ing been at the centre of whites' grand political project, now the inclu-sion of blacks was at the centre of blacks' central political purpose. It is this dialectic which explains the birth of African nationalism. It was born of racism authored by the white political elite.

The founders of the ANC understood the threat posed by divisions among Africans, which is why they worked hard to convince influen-tial African chiefs to be part of the new political formation. It would have been impossible, however, to secure the participation of ordinary Africans without going through chiefs, since Africans were at the time under the dominion of one chief or another.

The idea of bringing chiefs together to discuss common challenges facing Africans was an important beginning in the process of uniting the African people, and it explains how chiefs came to play an impor-tant role in the early life of the ANC. This move served to dilute the power of tribal identity and simultaneously lay the foundations for a bigger African consciousness. For the first time in the history of South Africa, an opportunity was created in 1912 for different African tribes to work towards a common ideal: the unity of the African people for political emancipation. This ideal would have been unimaginable when Shaka Zulu was terrorising other Africans during the Mfecane.

The role of the African intelligentsia was critical in developing a new African consciousness. Pixley ka Isaka Seme was particularly instrumental in this. He criss-crossed South Africa to convince African chiefs of the need to unite. Seme was an enlightened African nationalist. The question of African identity was at the centre of his political perspective. He had made this clear in 1906 at Columbia University when he delivered a memorable speech on 'The Regeneration of Africa' in which he declared: 'I am an African, and I set my pride in my race over against a hostile public opinion.'[20] Although there is a grievance that Seme presided over the weakening of the ANC in the 1930s, he is still acknowledged as its founder. Not only did he design the first structure of the organisation, he infused it with his African nationalist perspective. His ideological fingers left their marks on the name South African *Native National* Congress (our emphasis) (SANNC).

But the ANC's nationalism was not a virulent variant. From the outset, the organisation was driven by an inclusive perspective. The deputations dispatched by the ANC to London from 1914 onwards were not sent to make a case for the creation of an exclusively African government to govern South Africa; the main point was to protest against the exclusion of Africans from the Union government. The ANC pleaded with the British authorities for Africans to enjoy the same political rights enjoyed by whites in the Union of South Africa. It is anyone's guess as to how things would have panned out had the demands of the ANC been acceded to by Great Britain, following the first deputation of the ANC in 1914.

Even during periods of radicalism, such as the 1940s when the ANC Youth League (ANCYL) was formed, or the 1950s during the Defiance

Campaign, the ANC did not jettison its core character as an inclusive African nationalist organisation. This was despite the fact that Britain was not acceding to ANC demands. Not even the introduction of apartheid in 1948 managed to move the ANC to the extreme wing of African nationalism. The main demand remained: a racially inclusive democratic system in which all should have equal rights. The ANC's belief in the principle of equality was further concretised in the Freedom Charter, which was adopted on 26 June 1955 at a congress held in Kliptown and attended by South Africans of all races. The Charter declared unambiguously: 'The rights of the people shall be the same, regardless of race, colour or sex.'

This commitment to equality and the inclusive character of the ANC's nationalism did not please all in the organisation. There was a group that felt that the ANC's ideological orientation was not radical enough. This group was adamant that, since white settlers had dispossessed Africans of their land, through the Land Act of 1913 and other instruments, the Africans must not envision a future in which they would include whites in the governing of South Africa. The core demand of this group was for land to be returned to Africans, and for Africans to govern their own country. This was a radical political perspective: whites were settlers, and therefore had no right to play a role in the governing of South Africa.

Having failed to turn the ANC in the direction of an exclusionist African nationalism, this disgruntled group broke out of the ANC and formed the Pan Africanist Congress (PAC). This organisation was to be the embodiment of a more radical African nationalism, with the view, as set down in its constitution, to the 'establishment and maintenance of an Africanist socialist democracy'.[21] Throughout the life of the PAC, the question of land was to remain central to the political agenda of the organisation. Land remains a potent grievance today as land was a marker of subjugation during colonialism and under decades of NP rule.

The radicalism of the ANC, introduced by the ANCYL, combined with that of the PAC, led to the intensification of oppression by the apartheid regime. When these organisations intensified their defiance activities, the apartheid government resorted to killing people. One of the worst examples was when the police opened fire on unarmed protesters in Sharpeville on 21 March 1960, killing 69 people. The next step by the government was to ban all political parties fighting for the liberation of the African people. Leaders of these organisations who organised political activities underground were imprisoned for long periods of time, and their organisations operated underground and in exile until their unbanning in 1990.

During the years of underground politics (particularly in the 1970s) attempts were made in South Africa to resuscitate African nationalist politics. A key figure in this process was Steve Biko, who articulated a new Black Consciousness ideology. This was a daring undertaking, given the ferocity of the apartheid state, and Biko was eliminated in prison in 1977 by state security forces. Indeed, Biko's Black Consciousness ideology has been interpreted variously. There are some political organisations – such as the Azanian People's Organisation (AZAPO), the Socialist Party of Azania (SOPA), and others – that claim to be the true custodians of Biko's Black Consciousness. All these organisations are very determined in their own beliefs.

Since Biko died young, when Black Consciousness was still under development, many have appropriated his ideology and given it their own meanings. Other than AZAPO and SOPA, there are people who claim that, had Biko lived longer, he would have joined the ANC. The trouble is that Biko lies dead and silent in his grave. He cannot reply. All we know is the humanistic African nationalist character of his ideology that he himself articulated when he was still alive:

> *We must seek to restore to the black people a sense of the great stress*
> *we used to lay on the value of human relationships; to highlight the*

fact that in the pre-Van Riebeeck days we had a high regard for people, their property and for life in general.[22]

Here African nationalism stares us in the face. What is hard to decipher, though, is where exactly Biko's ideology lies on the continuum that stretches from the ANC's mild version to the PAC's extreme form of African nationalism.

Fundamentally, African nationalism, mild or virulent, is a product of and reaction to the politics of racial exclusion, introduced to South Africa by a long succession of white minority regimes – from the Dutch East India Company to British imperialism, from the Union government to apartheid. Had the human and political rights of the African people been promoted throughout the making of modern South Africa, it is doubtful whether African nationalism would have developed the way it did. History being what it is, however, no one can press a reverse button. Once the song has been played, it has been played.

Being the oldest liberation movement in Africa, and given that it has for decades withstood the stratagems of all manner of white supremacists, history has rewarded the ANC with the privilege of being the party that was at the forefront of the process of delivering South Africa from the despotism of race politics to democracy, even as F.W. de Klerk ingeniously worked to create his special place in South African history. The year 1994 is generally viewed as the culmination of the ANC's liberation gallantry. Looking from the vantage point of today, the ANC appears more like a historic necessity – a political party ordained by history to liberate the African people from the yoke of colonialism and apartheid. Historical fortunes do not necessarily guarantee future success, however. The important question was this: was the ANC ready to govern?

Chapter 2

READY TO GOVERN?

P rior to its unbanning in 1990, the ANC had for 30 years operated as an underground and exiled political movement. Its leaders and activists were scattered in many countries around the world. Those who were in South Africa were either prisoners or had to live like fugitives, dodging members of apartheid's security branch who hounded them like hungry lions intent on a kill. Under such difficult circumstances, the ANC did not have the luxury of spending time contemplating various permutations of a future government. Security was paramount. The intricacies of governing were on the back-burner.

Given the constrained political environment in which the ANC was forced to operate, it was to be expected that, upon its unbanning, the party would not be ready suddenly to govern so complex a country as South Africa. The party was quick to cast itself in a positive light, however, declaring itself 'Ready to Govern' through a package of policy proposals it released in 1992. By this time, it was more than obvious that the ANC was the political party poised to head up the first post-apartheid government. The party itself was conscious of this imminent political reality, and indeed mindful of the doubts and anxieties of local and international observers. It was hardly surprising then that the ANC hastened to make public 'a comprehensive set of guidelines highlighting the ANC's broad policy response to all the major areas of political, social and economic life'.[1] This was meant to communicate an emphatic message to the doubting Thomases of the world. But in truth, was the party really ready?

Historicist bravado

All political movements fighting for the liberation of the oppressed are driven by the desire and hope to emerge victorious from their struggles. Only insane people would risk their lives motivated by a deliberate intent to fail. But the desire to succeed is nothing more than what it is – a driving force behind action. In the context of political struggle, the actions of a liberation movement are not free from constraint. As liberation movements work to negate political oppression, forces of oppression at the same time work to undermine the objectives of those engaged in struggle.

Essentially, political struggle is the art of contradiction. It is not contradiction for its own sake, though; it is contradiction with a clear end in sight – the replacement of the repressive regime with the liberation forces. From their standpoint, the forces of repression are also engaged in the art of contradiction, plotting and working to sustain their hold on power, and to prevent the ascent of liberation forces to power. This process necessarily produces disequilibrium, operating like a see-saw, swinging up and down on the basis of momentary victories, either of the forces of liberation or those of repression. This period is fundamentally an era of disorder, a period whose very character is instability and uncertainty.

Political order, as American political scientist Francis Fukuyama observes, 'emerges as a result of the achievement of some equilibrium among the contending forces within a society'.[2] The timing of this is hard, if not impossible, to predict. Political struggles always involve the deployment of propaganda, either to sustain the spirit of the people

39

involved in the struggle or to intimidate the enemy into a position of surrender. Like any other liberation movement, the ANC also used propaganda to project itself as a side that was certain of victory, a side that was in control of destiny. But propaganda was not used exclusively by the ANC. For its part, the apartheid state also projected a face of eternal invincibility, even as those managing it knew all its vulnerabilities. The truth is that neither the ANC nor the forces of apartheid knew what would eventually happen, or how the end would ultimately play itself out. The events that unfolded in the last days of apartheid were in many ways a surprise, both to the ANC and to the apartheid government. Political analyst and former politician, the late Frederik van Zyl Slabbert could not be more apposite:

> For me it is quite clear that both De Klerk and the ANC faced the same set of circumstances. De Klerk genuinely thought he had the ANC at a disadvantage because of the fall of the [Berlin] Wall, and the ANC were reluctant and ambiguous about negotiations but saw how rapidly international support was flowing in their direction. The one [De Klerk] started negotiations and ended up the loser; the other [the ANC] reluctantly entered into negotiations and ended up the prime beneficiary.[3]

The ANC would, of course, contest this view, and claim to have been in control of the political events leading to the negotiations. In order to keep their members motivated, liberation movements claim to know how future political situations will unfold. Their approach is historicism, an ideological orientation cultivated from Marxism, which treats human societies like machines, the dynamics of which can be mastered to explain their twists and turns from beginning to end.

The philosopher Karl Popper offers a clearer definition of historicism, as a political doctrine that is premised on the idea that 'history is controlled by specific historical or evolutionary laws whose discovery would enable us to prophesy the destiny of man'.[4] Essentially, historicists believe that once they have mastered the discoverable laws of history, they can tell us what will happen in the future. This is a false ideology whose roots derive from Marxist propaganda.

Karl Marx was the arch historicist. He had the courage to predict the future, and to claim certitude. Marx sliced society into distinct social forces, whose characters and modi operandi were neatly explicable, to the point where Marx the analyst could predict how the fundamental contradiction between the proletariat and the bourgeoisie would eventually resolve itself, that is, in the victory of the working class and the defeat of capitalism, leading to socialism, which was the first stage towards communism.

It is a pity Marx was a mere mortal. If he lived at least for two centuries, how might he have rationalised why the United States of America has not yet seen the advent of socialism, even as it has undoubtedly reached the highest stage of capitalist development? So developed has capitalism been in the US that the country has, for most of the twentieth century, been exporting its model to most parts of the world, what Marx's own theoretical heir, Vladimir Lenin, describes as 'imperialism, the highest state of capitalism'.[5] In Marx's mechanistic conception, 'capitalist production begets, with the inexorability of a natural process, its own negation. This is the negation of the negation.'[6] Being the historicist that he was, Marx entitled the chapter in which he declared this pseudo-law 'The Historical Tendency of Capitalist Accumulation'.

If Karl Marx were alive today, we would ask him: 'Please tell us, Mr Marx, why is it that your prediction of the "negation of the negation" in "the historical tendency of capitalist accumulation" has, for more than a century of capitalist accumulation in the United States of America, not taken place?'

Even the cycles of economic collapse that have been witnessed since Marx made his prediction, failed to produce what he had in mind: 'namely co-operation and the possession in common of the land

and the means of production produced by labour itself'.[7] The Great Depression of the early 1930s certainly did not transform the world into Marx's supposedly inescapable upshot of capitalist accumulation. And following the 2008 global economic recession, not even the wave of bail-outs of collapsed private banks and other institutions by Western governments resulted in the permanent establishment of a new global Marxist regime of common ownership by labour of the land and the means of production. In short, Marx's historicism has been, at best, a barren theory. What Marx predicted never came to pass.

The problem with historicists is that they always have an excuse. Had Marx lived longer, he would most probably have manufactured an excuse to obfuscate the situation in the US. This is the fundamental defect of historicism as a pseudo-theory: it has scientific pretensions and at the same time it possesses the flexibility of a philosophy. Even with its scientific pretensions, it is impossible to pin historicism down – one minute it is here, and the next it is there. For Karl Marx to declare his 'historical tendency of capitalist accumulation', ascribing to it 'the inexorability of a natural process', was the worst form of pseudo-scientific ideology. Karl Popper was indeed correct:

> *Without waiting, passively, for repetitions to impress or impose regularities upon us, we actively try to impose regularities upon the world. We try to discover similarities in it, and to interpret it in terms of laws invented by us.*[8]

Of this crime, historicists are guilty. The ANC, inspired by pseudo-scientific Marxist theory, would like us to believe that it was in control of the political changes that led to the transition from apartheid to democracy in South Africa. We contend that this is a false, historicist narrative. The ANC, like De Klerk, did not know how the situation would play itself out. While liberation movements do exert pressure on despotic regimes, the outcome of their struggle and the timing of their ultimate success are not determined by the forces of liberation. These matters are resolved by a combination of complex and often unpredictable variables. When people engage in a liberation struggle, they generally do not know and are incapable of foreseeing the circumstances that will eventually facilitate the success of their mission. All they have is hope, sustained by daily survival.

Of those who congregated in Bloemfontein to form the ANC in 1912, not even the most gifted among them would have foreseen the advent of the Cold War. The Cold War was to become one of the most decisive factors in the conduct and destiny of the liberation struggle waged by the ANC. As we have suggested above, rational people who get involved in liberation struggles hope to succeed, and ultimately to enjoy the fruits of their efforts, but many die before they witness the fruits of their political labour. In the struggle, no one knows for sure what the end will look like or how it will unfold. The ANC could not have known what would happen, and how it would happen. Even as the ANC worked hard to weaken the apartheid state, its collapse still took many in the organisation by surprise. How, then, could the ANC declare itself 'Ready to Govern', when the collapse of apartheid came as a surprise? All this is a classic case of historicist bravado.

A tyranny of ideology

When we say the ANC was caught by surprise, we mean that before its unbanning, the party had not developed a detailed plan of how it would govern South Africa. For a liberation movement that had been engaged in the struggle since 1912, a period of 80 years, it is rather striking that it did not develop such a plan well before the 'Ready to Govern' campaigning in 1992. The real possibility of liberation seems to have dawned upon the ANC only in 1988, when, for the first time in its history, the party produced a document outlining its preferred constitutional guidelines for a democratic South Africa. In the document, the ANC says:

> *The Freedom Charter, adopted in 1955 by the Congress of the People at Kliptown near Johannesburg, was the first systematic statement in the history of our country of the political and constitutional vision of a free, democratic and non-racial South Africa.*[9]

What this means is that before 1955, the ANC had not systematically conceptualised and practically envisioned a free, democratic and non-racial South Africa. The party only operated on the basis of a gut feeling of freedom, without the coherence of thought expressed in a detailed document. Only after the adoption of the Freedom Charter did the ANC have an intellectually decent, documentary point of reference.

From nothing to the Freedom Charter, the ANC had indeed made a quantum leap in the field of policy formulation, even though some might suggest – rightly so – that the Freedom Charter was not drafted by the ANC, since the document was a product of the Congress of the People. What is more important, however, is that the party did adopt the Charter as its guiding policy platform. But still, the party did not have a detailed policy document, something approximating the 1992 'Ready to Govern' or the 1994 Reconstruction and Development Programme.

Just because the Freedom Charter did not contain a detailed blueprint for government – all it did was enunciate broad principles of an ideal society – this does not mean that its importance should be downplayed, and so this observation should not be misconstrued. But the Freedom Charter need not be made into a sacred document that is beyond criticism either. Those who gathered in Kliptown were human beings. What they produced cannot be held up as a blueprint for government for eternity. Nonetheless, placed in its socio-historical context, the Charter represented a ground-breaking political vision for

South Africa. Its significance did not only lie in the audacity of its political and economic demands, but also in the fact that it was a product of a broad spectrum of South African society. The legitimacy of the Freedom Charter dealt a moral blow to the apartheid state, both domestically and internationally.

What should have been done in the period following the adoption of the Freedom Charter was the conversion of the Charter by the ANC, if the organisation at the time indeed viewed itself as an alternative government, into a practical programme for a 'government-in-waiting'. There was ample time to do this. The party was more preoccupied with mythmaking, however, toying with the impossible task of taking over the country through the barrel of a gun. Even when it had operated underground for more than 20 years, the ANC still did not imagine itself as a government-in-waiting. There is no documentary evidence to demonstrate that they did.

Only in 1989, following the secret talks about talks that had been taking place in the second half of that decade between a small group of ANC leaders – led by Thabo Mbeki – and a small National Intelligence Service-directed team of Afrikaners – led by Professor Willie Esterhuyse – did the ANC realise the need to convert the Freedom Charter into a practical programme. Only in 1989 did the ANC declare: 'The stage is now approaching where the Freedom Charter must be converted from a vision for the future into a constitutional reality.'[10] When was 'the stage' going to come, or for how long would it keep approaching? The ANC did not know.

It would have been embarrassing, of course, for the ANC elite to admit to intellectual limitations when the majority of the people had effectively delegated all the thinking to them, viewing them as revolutionary gods. So the pretence and posturing had to go on with the hope that, after taking charge of the levers of power, all would be crystal clear.

But what would the ANC have done had it anticipated the timing of its unbanning well in advance, or had it anticipated its rise to power, say, ten years before 1990? Most probably, the document 'Ready to Govern', or a version thereof, would have been produced in the early 1980s, even if it meant keeping it under wraps until the party was unbanned. This would have had positive implications for the preparedness of the party come 1994. The party would have had the time to plan many aspects of a democratic government in detail. It would have had the time to learn from other democracies in anticipation of its own tasks in a democratic context. Not only would the party have refined its policy plans thoroughly, by then it would have also entertained likely scenarios for a future South Africa, an important exercise for a government-in-waiting. The ANC did not engage in this exercise before 1990.

Because the ANC was taken by surprise, it miscalculated in certain areas which would affect the party in the future. Among the important areas of miscalculation was the field of economic policy. In the 'Ready to Govern' document, the ANC provided a broad sketch of its economic policy. Given the all-encompassing nature of such a document – which was meant to reflect on social, political and economic aspects of the ANC's future government – it was impossible to furnish full details of what a future ANC-managed South African economy would entail. In the document, the ANC could deal with the economy in merely broad terms. The party promised to implement an economic policy with 'two principal components':

- Redistribution programmes to meet the basic needs of our people. A priority in this regard will be the provision of basic services, affordable housing and infrastructure ...

- The restructuring of the South African economy on the basis of new, comprehensive and sustained growth and development strategies in all sectors of the economy.[11]

Given the material dispossession of black people by centuries of colonialism and apartheid, it is not difficult to understand why, from the outset, the ANC adopted a redistributive posture. This redistributive orientation was articulated in detail in the ANC's first economic policy, the Reconstruction and Development Programme (RDP), adopted in 1994. The policy was developed under the influence of Cosatu, so the RDP became very popular among the rank and file of the ANC. Its crafters were exuberant and ambitious. Paragraph 1.1.1. made the statement:

> *The RDP is an integrated, coherent socio-economic policy framework.*
> *It seeks to mobilise all our people and our country's resources toward*
> *the final eradication of apartheid and the building of a democratic,*
> *non-racial and non-sexist future.*

All this is perfectly understandable, except that it was a product of naivety and demonstrated a lack of appreciation for the complexities ahead of the first ANC-led government. This naivety was itself the result of two related things: firstly, an insufficient attention to facts about the South African economy at the time; and secondly, the tyranny of ideology.

What facts did the enthusiasts of redistribution ignore at the time? In sum, the ANC was to inherit a bankrupt economy. The South African economy had not recovered from the global economic downturn precipitated by the oil crisis of 1973. The rest of the 1970s was a turbulent period internally in South Africa. First was the 1973 workers' strike, and in the same decade, there was the 1976 Soweto uprising. The response of the state was to ratchet up the militarisation of the state, which placed a further strain on the economy. As Terreblanche observes: 'The NP government increased its military spending quite drastically, from 2.2% in 1972 to almost 10% in 1989.'[12] For 20 years since 1974, the economy *stagflated*, registering a negligible annual average growth of 1.7%. This

47

could not sustain the ever-growing militarisation of the state. Adding economic sanctions to this was like pouring fuel onto the flames that finally melted apartheid.

In addition to all this, De Klerk and his henchmen depleted state coffers towards the end of apartheid in the early 1990s. Terreblanche comments: 'During F W de Klerk's tenure of the presidency from 1989 until 1994, the government deficit increased from R91.2 billion to R237 billion (in current prices).'[13]

Where did all this money go? While the ANC was preaching a redistribution-first message in the early 1990s, it seems that De Klerk and his henchmen were busy milking the state. In the enthusiasm that accompanied the workshops and conferences that were hammering out the details that went into the RDP document, there was no room for probably the most important question: where would the ANC get the money to pay for the laundry list of promises it was making to the people in the RDP? In this the ANC leaders were not only complacent but they showed poor judgement.

As the ANC and its alliance partners were busy developing the RDP, its activists were under the tyranny of the ideology of redistribution. The excitement generated by the unbanning of the liberation movement created expectations of a dream soon to be fulfilled. The RDP was crafted as though the document would have magical powers instantaneously to undo the damage created by more than three centuries of colonialism and apartheid. The ideological mood was that of instant revolution, propelled by an all-powerful political bulldozer that could crush any neo-liberal attempt to project RDP promises as unrealistic. The RDP was thus viewed as a magic wand that could turn a rock into bread, mud huts into decent houses, water from a dirty stream into purified tap water – almost instantaneously.

The aphorism that 'If you forget that you are poor, your conditions will remind you' could not be more true. It did not take long before the ANC woke up. Hardly two years following the adoption of the RDP, some of the ANC thinkers realised that the party could not distribute what it did not have. Access to state information also revealed that the popular belief by the ANC that the state was very rich, and that, if it so wished, it could end poverty in one fell swoop was an illusion. In a year or so, it became clear to ANC representatives in government that De Klerk and his fellow apartheid henchmen had bankrupted the state.

What, then, was to be done? The ANC's culture has been one of debate. When confronted with the reality of a bankrupt state, it was to be expected that a debate would ensue to discuss and decide the way forward. The storm of economic policy debate that proceeded to engulf the ANC and its tripartite alliance partners, two years into government, essentially produced two camps: the first camp could be dubbed the 'austerity crusade' and the second the 'radical crusade'.

The 'austerity crusade' was led by Thabo Mbeki. This group advocated for deferring the social benefits listed in the RDP in order to prioritise the macro-economic stabilisation of the economy. The idea was that, in time, once the economy had stabilised, and growth had been achieved, it would be feasible for the state to provide the goodies of the RDP. This was the essence of the Growth, Employment and Redistribution Programme (Gear). Members of the 'austerity crusade' were terrified of debt, believing that borrowing would diminish the fiscal independence of the South African state. For this group, 'the choice was either to borrow more and end up, begging bowl in hand, at the International Monetary Fund and World Bank, or to reduce the budget deficit while reprioritising expenditure'.[14] The 'austerity crusade' wanted to avoid the easy path of borrowing.

For members of the 'radical crusade', Gear represented a neo-liberal offensive against the masses of the poor who could not afford to wait for the promised fruits of Gear to trickle down. Champions of this group included Blade Nzimande, secretary-general of the SACP and Cosatu. The radicals believed that economic growth was possible through redistribution.

49

To say that members of the radical offensive hated Gear would be an understatement; they were up in arms opposing it and all sorts of labels were coined to ridicule members of the 'austerity crusade'. In time, the labels congealed into one lasting, derogatory description: 'the 1996 Class Project'. To tell someone they were a member of 'the 1996 Class Project' was considered among the worst insults in Cosatu and the SACP – it was like being labelled a spy during the liberation struggle.

For our purposes, it does not matter who was right or wrong between members of the 'austerity' or 'radical' crusades; the point we make is that this debate should have taken place long before the ANC ascended to power. The fact that, up until 1994, the ANC was under the impression that the state it was set to inherit was economically in excellent shape and that, upon its ascent to power, it would immediately be in a position to deliver everything on the RDP list of goodies, is a sign of naivety and unreadiness to govern. The U-turn made only two years into power – in 1996 – from the RDP to Gear can only be evidence of an organisation that did not know what was happening in the real world of statecraft. It also failed to seek out talent – the best and the brightest in society – to help it with technocratic capacities. Instead, the ANC relied largely on the very same people who had been feeding on Marxist jargon while in exile or on Robben Island. An attitude of arrogance – 'we have enough capable cadres schooled in the National Democratic Revolution in our movement' – prevailed. Yet the evidence of confusion was everywhere in abundance.

The actual field of governing is not the terrain of pure ideology. The world of ideology is not very different from that of hallucinations, where the mind derives gratification from the fantasy of the abstract possibilities availed by the experience of floating in mid-air. Ideologues and fantasists are the same; what their minds can visualise is what they think can be done. Ultimately, it is before reality that all dreamers must kneel. In the world of fantasy, RDP goodies were easy to enumerate, but they had to be paid for with money generated from the real world of financial constraints. It was in the real world where the ANC woke up.

Dreams are the stuff of slumber. Only in death do people sleep forever. When you are asleep, you are bound to wake up and face reality eventually. Similarly, the naive expectation of ANC activists in the early 1990s that the RDP would magically deliver all that colonialism and apartheid had robbed from the majority of South Africans did not last long. The reality of incumbency shook the ANC from its slumber, and the party realised that a list of goodies is all very well, but it is nothing if it is not accompanied by the availability of money to buy them.

Economics was not the only area of slumber for the ANC. Corruption was another. It is hard to find a serious document developed by the ANC before 1990 dealing with corruption, a document to prove that the party was alive to the corrosive dangers of corruption to itself or to an ANC-run government. This is despite many incidences of corruption the ANC had already had to confront amongst its leaders and rank-and-file in exile. In the 'Ready to Govern' document, it is striking that not a single section is devoted to corruption. As the ANC was dreaming about the future in the early 1990s and before, only angels must have appeared in its sleep. It never occurred to the ANC that venality could sprout under its governance, yet in exile corruption was not uncommon.

That Jacob Zuma is what many would consider a man of simple mind is well known. But sometimes his simple mind manufactures very strange religious jokes. Consider, for example, what he told ANC supporters as recently as February 2011:

> When you vote for the ANC, you are also choosing to go to heaven. When you don't vote for the ANC you should know that you are choosing that man who carries a fork ... who cooks people.[15]

The ANC's dreams were nothing more than dreams. Some of the party's trusted angels, such as Tony Yengeni, were convicted of corruption, and ended up mingling with criminals in a place associated with sins – jail. In 1994 Yengeni was convicted for accepting a discount on a luxury car, which essentially constituted a bribe. Yet he had been one of the great dreamers of the future who in 1992 had drafted 'Ready to Govern' as if the ANC *were* heaven, fortified against infiltration from the other side, the side where Jacob Zuma's 'man who carries a fork' reigned supreme. The cloud of corruption scandals which hangs over Zuma's head today suggests that Zuma and the 'man who carries a fork' may actually be residents of the same Great Republic of Corruption – the ANC.

Meanwhile, Thabo Mbeki had an interesting explanation for why some of his ANC comrades are corrupt:

> *Liberation from a dictatorship inevitably also entails corruption ... People who have been oppressed and disadvantaged economically argue that they lost a great deal in the past. Hence they believe they are entitled to 'make up for it'.*[16]

Mbeki was right. In 2007, Smuts Ngonyama, then head of Mbeki's office in the ANC, infamously told the world: 'I did not join the struggle to be poor.'[17] This is not the imaginary world of dreamers; it is the real world of corruptible souls, who are also found in the ANC.

There are indications that the ANC is waking up to the dangers of corruption. There is hardly a speech by the ANC president, or an assessment report by the party's secretary-general, that does not allude to the perils of corruption, both for the party and for the state. What is still missing is firm action by those in charge. This, it appears, could be explained on the basis of the fact that those in charge were themselves accused of corruption. The fact that they are in charge makes it difficult for the public to get to the bottom of the allegations or for ordinary party members to resist the temptations of corruption. Is it not naive to expect a police officer accused of corruption to arrest himself? We reflect on the fatal impact of corruption on the ANC in Chapter 4.

A glorious start towards disaster

Dreams notwithstanding, the ANC appeared, in 1994, to have a glorious start. Its articulation of the hopes of South Africans and its message of reconciliation were inspiring. The commitment of liberation movements with Marxist backgrounds to freedom is always suspect, however. Marxist organisations tend to adopt a commandist approach to governance, inspired by such Marxist concepts as 'the dictatorship of the proletariat', 'democratic centralism', or 'rule by a collective' – all concepts that are meant to both obfuscate or to enable privileged members of a faction to impose their will. The record of the Communist Party in the former Soviet Union casts a shadow of doubt upon socialist parties that take over governments all over the world. Given its historic alliance with the South African Communist Party, and the latter having been part of the world socialist movement, the ANC was not spared the cynicism and half-heartedness that generally greet socialist-oriented governments the world over. And, given the brutality to which black people had been subjected by successive minority white regimes, most observers found it hard to believe the sincerity of the ANC's commitment to reconciliation.

To the disbelief of many, the ANC did stick to its word. Nelson Mandela led his party and the new democratically elected government down the path of peace, reconciliation and multiracialism. In the main, the first five years of ANC government were about two strategic tasks: firstly, reconciliation; and, secondly, replacing the mountain of apartheid legislation with laws in harmony with the newly adopted human-rights-based Constitution.

Imperfect as the Truth and Reconciliation Commission (TRC) may have been, it did serve as a valve through which the nation's collective anguish escaped. Even if it did not provide answers to all who had questions, the TRC was a grand symbolic gesture of national healing and forgiveness. All this happened under the leadership of the ANC.

By the time Mandela handed over the baton to Thabo Mbeki in 1999, a great deal of work, albeit imperfect, had already been done in defusing tensions among South Africans from different racial backgrounds. It was now credible that something of a new, 'rainbow' South African nation was possible. Almost all apartheid laws that did not conform to the new constitutional order had been repealed or amended accordingly.

What remained daunting was the task of addressing the poor socio-economic conditions of the black majority. As historian Neville Alexander poignantly observed:

> It is common cause in South Africa that unless a radical redistribution of material resources is realised within the lifetime of the present generation, all the glib rhetoric of social transformation, National Democratic Revolution, and African Renaissance, will come to mock their authors and exponents in years to come.[18]

The new president was aware of how difficult this was going to be. In the late 1980s, during the secret talks about talks, Mbeki had sounded a stern warning:

> The political process of transition to an inclusive democracy with international status should not be too difficult ... The socio-economic transition process, though, is the more complex. There is terrible poverty, and the legacy of apartheid is visible everywhere. There are also high material expectations on the part of the oppressed. The gap between the rich and poor is massive. How are we going to integrate 30 million blacks, mostly poor, in an economic process that is currently controlled by a rich, white elite?[19]

It is little wonder that the economic question became one of Mbeki's obsessions. While most whites did not like Mbeki's characterisation of the economic question fundamentally as a racial matter, no one has produced evidence to prove that Mbeki was wrong about the economy, before and during his time as president of South Africa, being under the control of 'a rich, white elite'. The serious crime committed by Mbeki was that, by emphasising the racial question, he appeared like someone intent on deviating from Mandela's 'rainbow-ism', which was essentially a psycho-social approach to the national question. In the five years of his presidency, Mandela's main achievement was the dilution of racial hatred among South Africans. His major weakness, though, was that his over-moralising was at the expense of the more serious question of the economic disempowerment of the black majority. This is what Mbeki sought to correct. But did Mbeki's ANC succeed?

If we judge Mbeki on the basis of his own concern – 'the integration of 30 million blacks, mostly poor, into an economic process that is owned by a rich white elite' – he has clearly failed. By the time he was booted out of government in 2008, unemployment was 21.9%, while 36.4% of South Africans were living on less than $2.50 (R23.75) per day, which was at the time South Africa's poverty baseline.

This, however, does not mean that the ANC did absolutely nothing to improve the lives of the poor. As the ANC-led government itself acknowledged:

> *The single most important driver of the decline in poverty is government's social security assistance programme ... The rapid expansion of the social security system lies at the heart of the growth in expenditure levels of the poor.*[20]

In the year 2014, about 17 million South Africans are receiving social grants. The backlog notwithstanding, the overall record of the government in the provision of electricity, clean running water, housing and other social needs is impressive. Of concern, however, is the future sustainability of a nanny state for South Africa. How many more poor South Africans can the state afford to pull into its already over-stretched safety net?

Thabo Mbeki was also concerned about the massive gap between the rich and the poor, yet he failed to halve the level of inequality during his time as president of the Republic. In 1996, when Gear was intro-duced, South Africa had a Gini coefficient (which is an internationally accepted measure of inequality) of 0.69. By the time Mbeki left govern-ment in 2008, this had come down only marginally – to 0.67. While Mbeki presided over the longest period of sustained economic growth, it was not the kind of growth that integrated millions of unskilled South Africans into the formal economy. Between 2003 and 2007, the economy was growing at an annual rate of between 4% and 5%. The prime beneficiaries of the jobs created were members of the black mid-dle class, whose lives improved dramatically.

When the gloss of economic growth was wiped out by the experience of the 2008 global economic recession, the fundamental core of South Africa's post-apartheid economy was exposed badly. What remained was what has historically been the crisis of our country: an extractive economy that enriches a few and impoverishes the majority.

In the early days of the development of the mining industry, in the second half of the nineteenth century, the South African economy was designed to enrich a few English moguls, and to impoverish the rest. From 1910 to the end of apartheid, the grand plan was to enrich white people, and to impoverish the rest. The upshot of the first two decades of ANC rule has been the enrichment of whites and a relatively few blacks, and the impoverishment of the rest.

The worst thing about the ANC is that the blacks it has been enrich-ing are not really engaged in production; they wear suits and wait for deals and easy money from their real bosses – white entrepreneurs. Blacks who have benefited from Black Economic Empowerment (BEE) schemes are, in the main, politically connected to the ANC. Some cronies have also milked it via the development finance institutions meant to increase the participation of blacks in economic activity. In truth, BEE has in our opinion been a redistribution scheme for ANC leaders and cronies; the word 'black' has been used to legitimise what in reality is a sordid money affair. To encourage them to co-operate in this dirty scheme, 17 million poor blacks are 'bribed' with social grants, grants that will never dig these poor black people out of their dark pit of poverty. So while the social structure has its origins in the apartheid order, the slow pace at changing it is attributable to bad policies and wrong priorities of the ANC government. It is as if the ANC is intent on colluding with the past as a means of keeping its nationalism aflame.

Beneath the patina of success during the Mbeki years, rot was festering. Because of Mbeki's personal overbearing image of an intellectual, it appeared as though the government was managed by great intellectuals who were all pushing the state machinery in the direction of excellence. This was not the case. There was a thick layer of mediocrity and incompetence below the glitter of Mbeki's cultivated intellectual persona, and this layer was busy sapping the vitality of the state.

In fact, local government in South Africa began collapsing under Mbeki. It was Mbeki who introduced the hit-and-run approach of the national government to local government, under the codename 'Project Consolidate'. This was an intervention by the presidency in municipalities that had almost collapsed. If local government under Mbeki was a model of success, what was Project Consolidate for?

Since Mbeki's departure from government, the situation seems to have gone from bad to worse. As we will point out in Chapter 4, the Zuma administration is more brazen in wasting state resources. When Zuma took over, he ballooned his cabinet at the expense of the taxpayer. There are some ministries in which nobody knows what occurs on a daily basis. The Minister for Women, Children and Persons with Disabilities, Lulama Xingwana, often sounds like an NGO activist, calling upon judges to deny bail to suspects, as if she does not operate in a cabinet governed by the same South African Constitution that declares suspects innocent until proven guilty. If the world revolved around her wishes, Xingwana's political boss, Jacob Zuma, would be languishing in jail, for he would have been declared 'guilty until proven innocent'. But Xingwana is not the only redundant minister. The Ministry of Economic Development seems to be another, a think-tank whose products exist only in the heads of its officials.

Under Jacob Zuma, we have seen the highest number of provincial departments collapsing, necessitating interventions by a national government whose capacity to deliver is already doubtful. Since 1994, we had not witnessed a situation where the national government had to intervene in five provinces at the same time. This happened for the first time under Jacob Zuma. It was also under Zuma's administration that government failed to deliver textbooks to schools in Limpopo, something that has projected South Africa's image onto world screens as a banana republic. Under Zuma, corruption scandals in government have become normal. Citizens are no longer alarmed by wrongdoing – it is the order of the day.

In the area of safety and security, recent developments suggest a government that is becoming more incompetent and dangerous. Whenever there are protests by members of the public, we almost certainly expect citizens to die at the hands of the police. The worst example of this trend was the Marikana massacre of 2012, when 34 miners were mowed down with live bullets by a police force commanded by a grossly inexperienced general, Riah Phiyega. Only in a bizarre country such as South Africa can you have a person who has had no experience in the security sector overnight becoming the head of the police force. When criminals watch such a spectacle, they must surely laugh.

The general management of public institutions by the ANC government leaves much to be desired. Parliament seems to have become a rubber stamp for decisions taken in Luthuli House. Parliamentarians of the ruling party defer to the executive. They do not hold the executive to account because they depend on the party for placement on the parliamentary list in anticipation of the next elections. So they know how to behave in order to please the party bosses. The South African Broadcasting Corporation (SABC) limps from crisis to crisis. State-owned companies are often in the news for all the wrong reasons. If they are not explaining some scandal, they are justifying why they need to be bailed out by government. In 2013 we witnessed high drama at South African Airways when members of its board resigned as a result of interference by the Minister of Public Enterprises.

Given all this, the question again arises: was the ANC really ready to govern? While the party may claim its glorious beginning in the early years of its government, profiting morally from the magnanimity of Nelson Mandela, later developments suggest a party drifting towards disaster, a party consumed by corruption within its ranks, factionalism, mediocrity and lack of vision. All this does not suggest a party that was ready to govern – not in the long term. Apart from the tens of billions of rand that are mismanaged or effectively, in our opinion, stolen in the public service from municipality level to national government, the party has also failed to deliver on its promise for a better life for all. Evidence is mounting that the ANC was far from ready to govern. Hopefully, history will prove us wrong.

Chapter 3

FALSE OPTIMISM?

G iven South Africa's prolonged history of racial discrimination, it is hardly surprising that the country's transition from apartheid to democracy generated anxiety. The prospect of creating a new society, where black and white people would live in harmony, seemed at the beginning a quixotic ideal. There was the fear that, having endured centuries of dehumanising discrimination under white rule, the black majority would be driven by the visceral urge to mete out vengeance and resort to violence to rectify the wrongs of the past. Radical nationalism was expected to be in full swing before very long. This was an expectation that was born of a subliminal recognition of the injustices of the apartheid system and the resentment they invoked.

There were some in the disappearing political infrastructure of apartheid who had forebodings about South Africa's own version of the Nuremberg trials, where those who were found guilty of crimes against humanity would countenance vengeful punishment for their sins. Thabo Mbeki remarked that the ANC leadership eschewed the Nuremberg-style tribunal in order to give peace and stability a chance.[1] It needs underscoring, though, that it would have been nearly impossible to gain consensus for such a trial. As Neville Alexander points out: 'The conditions for such a tribunal did not exist in South Africa, since the National Party had not been defeated militarily.[2] Nevertheless, ordinary white citizens were uncertain of their future in the country. A few of them emigrated to Australia and other Western countries in fear of an imaginary calamity to come.

Placed in perspective, intimations of retribution were not out of keeping with the dominant spirit of the twentieth century's bloody realism. The wars of the West almost always ended up with victors and losers – the latter would be punished severely for their sins. British philosopher Isaiah Berlin characterises the past century as 'the most terrible century in Western history'.[3] Indeed, the forces of history did succeed in drawing South Africa into the vortex of Western wars. In both world wars, our country was not an insignificant player. In the First World War, for example, 9 000 South African combatants were killed and 12 000 were wounded.[4] European and world wars typically ended with the psychological ascendance of notions of conquerors and the vanquished.

Unlike in Nuremberg, South Africa managed to hold back the gathering clouds of Armageddon. The violence of the early 1990s notwithstanding, the full-blown civil war many people expected never happened. Courage and magnanimity joined hands to produce what is now known as the South African miracle. The decision by former President F.W. de Klerk to free political prisoners and unban the liberation movements will certainly go down in history among the most outstanding acts of courage. Nelson Mandela's choice of forgiveness and reconciliation, after spending 27 years in an apartheid prison, was magnanimity beyond limit. All this planted the seeds of enthusiasm about the future of South Africa, and blunted the blades of Afro-pessimism that were more than ready to cut the last thread of hope. But was this hope a mere case of false optimism?

A leadership equal to the task

The progression of events alongside the spirit of reconciliation happened, in the main, due to the historic fortune South Africa had at the time of a leadership that was suited for the political task at hand. As individuals Nelson Mandela and F.W. de Klerk were not so superhuman as to be able to solve every big or small problem that accompanied the precarious transition to democracy in South Africa. Neither did they necessarily enjoy an untrammelled space in which to do as they wished. There were factions of hotheads in both the parties they represented which needed persuading and convincing. In wider society, there were bigger social forces that had their own agencies, forces motivated by their narrow expectations, and elements that did not appreciate the straightjacketing effects of formal political structures. On the side of the oppressed black majority, dramatic change for the better had to happen now. And, on the part of white South Africans, care had to be taken not to compromise their future security and existing privileges.

Mandela and De Klerk operated within political parties that had their own agendas. The ANC was a political party with its own decision-making structures and processes. These were not entirely controlled by Mandela himself. As Thabo Mbeki told Willie Esterhuyse during their secret negotiations in the early 1990s, Mandela 'was running huge political risks among his people, especially the new generation'.[5] There were people in the ANC who were very concerned about Mandela's over-extension of the olive branch. Radical communists such as Harry Gwala, Chris Hani and others were impatient. The radical elements within the ANC would have preferred a military takeover by MK, the ANC's military wing. To this group, the idea of negotiating with the 'enemy' seemed like capitulation and a betrayal of the cause of the National Democratic Revolution.

Similarly, not all in the then ruling National Party were enthusiastic about De Klerk's political adventurism. To hawks in the apartheid security forces, the possibility of handing over power to a black government which had not militarily defeated apartheid was absolute madness. So strong was this feeling that, 15 years into democracy, Gerard Ludi, a man who spent decades of his life playing a central role in apartheid's anti-liberation movement espionage, could not forgive Mandela:

> I cannot share this feeling of Mandela's sainthood until he has apologised to the tens of thousands of innocent South African [sic] that he and his fellow Marxist revolutionaries planned to maim and murder in the planned revolution.[6]

If Ludi could say this in 2011, the intensity of the anti-Mandela sentiment among apartheid's securocrats cannot be underestimated.

That Mandela and De Klerk were able to surmount the internal political pressures within their respective political parties and among black and white South Africans is a mark of epic leadership. There is, however, a subtle gradation of the specific roles played by the two leaders in the narratives that explain the transition in South Africa. Even as both leaders were joint recipients of the Nobel Peace Prize in 1993, and stood shoulder to shoulder during transition, Mandela's shoulder should stand a little higher than De Klerk's in post-apartheid political morality. One only needs to decode the praises sung for both leaders to detect this.

Reconciliatory sentimentalism has rendered it almost profane to remind people that F.W. de Klerk was once a leader of apartheid. Public discourse in post-apartheid South Africa has been content with the reborn image of De Klerk as a progressive statesman. He quickly transformed in the eyes of many to a courageous leader who assisted us to cross the Rubicon. This image is not wrong, but it is as true as the fact that De Klerk was once a leader of apartheid. In fact, it is the unstated acknowledgement of this fact that makes the songs sung about De Klerk's greatness not quite so loud nor joyous as those sung for Mandela.

Even as there were white people like Gerard Ludi, who refused to forgive Nelson Mandela because he did not apologise for his activities during the liberation struggle, the majority of white South Africans adored Mandela. That a black 'terrorist', jailed for 27 years by a white apartheid state, could come out of prison and preach forgiveness was unbelievable to most white South Africans.

When the 95-year-old Mandela passed on in December 2013, there was an outpouring of emotions from across the world.

In a transcendental sense, Mandela represented the meeting point between the fundamental humanity of black and white people in South Africa. It is not an exaggeration to suggest that he did so for all humanity the world over.

Whatever judgements people may prefer, the leadership role played by De Klerk and Mandela in the transition from apartheid to democracy in South Africa cannot be downplayed, especially the crucial role they each played in calming passions and stabilising the country. Beyond stabilisation and managing the soft issues, however, much more was needed to improve the socio-economic conditions of South Africans. This said, it cannot be refuted that the process of negotiations, which De Klerk and Mandela led, and which culminated in the first democratic elections in South Africa, and the subsequent new constitutional framework, lifted the national mood.

Of course it was not all smooth sailing and the transition remained tenuous in many respects. Hostilities continued unabated in KwaZulu-Natal. In this part of the country, the relations between the ANC and the IFP were frosty. A series of peace initiatives were set in motion by leaders of the three main parties – the ANC, NP and IFP – with the realisation across the political spectrum that working for peace and stability was going to be a crucial foundation for the new South Africa. Mandela's commitment to forgiveness and the coining by Archbishop

Desmond Tutu of the description 'rainbow nation' were inspirational. In these circumstances the power of reason was able to prevail over jingoistic passions.

What became clear during the transition was that leadership and values have a shaping impact on the psyche of nations. These can inspire hope in a way that generates momentum for social and economic progress. American historian and political scientist James MacGregor Burns would refer to this kind of leadership as 'transforming leadership', whereby 'one or more persons *engage* with others in such a way that leaders and followers raise one another to higher levels of motivation and morality'.[7] South Africa was fortunate to have such leadership suited for the task at hand during its transition to democracy.

Where are the economic fruits?

While Mandela and De Klerk must be credited, and deservedly so, for the peace and reconciliation that marked the transition to democracy in South Africa, the majority of the oppressed black people needed peace and reconciliation to be accompanied by economic benefits. Political freedom without economic fruits would be meaningless for the dispossessed masses. This is why Indian economist and Nobel laureate Amartya Sen thinks of 'freedom as development' – a concept he uses to refer both to income improvement and enhancement of capabilities of the citizens.[8] A hungry person who is politically free is as good as unfree. The ANC has for decades shared this conception. The socio-economic core of the party's historic promise was set down in the Freedom Charter: 'The national wealth of our country, the heritage of South Africans, shall be restored to the people.'[9] Thus, when poor South Africans heeded Mandela's call to be patient, they did so anticipating economic dividends to flow from the ensuing peace and stability. But, unfortunately, people have waited for far too long. Instead

65

of witnessing the trickling down of wealth as promised and expected, 20 years into democracy they continue to associate economic privilege with whiteness and poverty with blackness. The only black people they see enjoying economic prosperity are the same faces that belong to the BEE elite who have close ties with the ruling party, the ANC.

One of the myths that has been peddled by the ANC to convince South Africans that their lives will change for the better under its rule is the notion of a developmental state. It has featured consistently as part of the party's rhetorical flourish. It is meant to give the impression that we are not far from turning South Africa into a land of milk and honey. Whenever the economic results show evidence to the contrary, the usual and increasingly tired explanation is that the legacy of colonialism and apartheid cannot be eradicated overnight.

This over-used excuse is not convincing. There are other countries in the world which also suffered from economic backwardness or under colonialism but who did not cry foul or allow themselves to get stuck in the past. It took South Korea three decades of sustained economic growth to become a model of development. When it started out, South Korea had the same level of development as Ghana. It was largely agrarian and had just a rudimentary industrial infrastructure, bequeathed by Japan's colonialism. Like many countries in the developing world, including South Africa, South Korea, too, had suffered the brutality of colonialism. As political scientist Atul Kohli points out: 'Japanese colonial impact was more intense [and] more brutal'.[10] Like all colonial powers, Japan was motivated by political dominance and economic extraction.

The politico-economic story of South Africa is not dissimilar to that of South Korea. Just as South Korea benefited from Japan's legacy of an industrialising economy, South Africa, too, had some economic inheritance from its colonial past. By 1994, the country had an organised bureaucracy, albeit plagued by inefficiencies and corruption, a thriving mining industry, a decent but insufficient infrastructure, and aspects of manufacturing that had established the basis for industrial growth.

Poverty and unemployment are not curses peculiar to South Africa; other countries in the world have experienced this challenge. There are countries that have made progress in this regard. In little under three decades, the Chinese government has managed to lift 400 million people out of poverty. In more recent times, Brazil, through its social policy tool called Bolsa Família, has lifted roughly 20 million people out of poverty, and reduced income inequalities. This is not to suggest that the ANC should have copied the strategies of South Korea, China or Brazil, or that all of this is an easy task, but to demonstrate that making economic advances is possible and excuses about the length of colonialism are as pathetic as they are shameful.

Without telling us how long it still requires to turn the country around, the ANC pleads for more time in power – perhaps as long as the National Party government had. The ANC insists on being measured by the standards of the apartheid government, by stating that it is better than its predecessors rather than by proving how it uses its position of power to bring about change in people's livelihoods. Interestingly, the longer the ANC stays in power, the more, it appears, the country confronts the tough realities of a slow-growing economy, decline in the quality of education, and deepening social inequalities. In fact, it is under ANC rule that South Africa took over the inglorious mantle from Brazil as the most unequal country in the world.

Yet the ANC has never stopped dishing out economic promises and, whenever there are elections ahead, the slogans are punched out by the ANC's slogan factory: 'Halving poverty and unemployment by 2014', 'A better life for all' and 'Job creation' – specious slogans at best.

In the 2009 general election, when it was patently clear that South Africans were growing increasingly impatient, the ANC shifted to a more cunning slogan: 'Together we can do more'. At this point, the party had realised that its messianic, distributive posture could no longer be sustained in a political environment of poor citizens who were tired of waiting. Thus it constructed a slogan which also placed a responsibility on citizens, inviting people to act 'together' with the ANC to 'do more'. This left enough manoeuvring space for the party in later years to turn around and say, 'The ANC did its part; citizens did not.'

What makes the notion of a developmental state particularly attractive to South Africa's governing elite is that it obfuscates. 'Developmental state' is a catch-all phrase that can mean just about anything under the sun. It also serves to justify the long stay of political elites in power, since the nebulousness of a 'developmental state' can be pursued forever. It is nothing more than an elusive ideal that citizens may endlessly pursue.

Often overlooked is the fact that the very notion of a 'developmental state' – with its Asian lineage – has an authoritarian core. American author and academic Chalmers Johnson, who is widely credited for coining the concept, observed that, the

> source of authority in the developmental state is not one of Weber's 'holy trinity' of traditional, rational-legal, and charismatic sources of authority. It is rather revolutionary authority: the authority of a people committed to the transformation of social, political, or economic order.[11]

This is mythical stuff when transposed to South Africa, where the ruling party reincarnates as an embodiment of the 'people' with a revolutionary task that should brook no opposition.

Much talk about the developmental state in South Africa is in a sense subliminally desirous of the political culture that prevailed in the prototypes of such a state. When Japan's developmental state was born, it was authoritarian. Similarly, the nature of the state in Korea, especially during the high industrialisation phase in the 1970s, was authoritarian. Taiwan was under martial law from 1949 until 1987.[12]

These states undertook their industrial development and economic reform processes under paternalistic circumstances, where there was considerable unity between the state and society, with the individual interests subsumed under those of the collective.[13] Even political economists such as Sampie Terreblanche, who are critical of the ANC's economic policies, contemplate that, perhaps, a benevolent dictatorship could have helped establish conditions of shared prosperity in the South Africa of the early 1990s, thus viewing the ANC's failure as a result of simply having made wrong choices.[14]

The ANC has also failed to use public education as a vehicle to rescue masses of black people from poverty. Only a few citizens have managed to escape destitution. That education is the surest way out of poverty for the children of the poor cannot be over-emphasised. As Amartya Sen observes, what placed China ahead of India in respect of poverty alleviation was education:

> The social backwardness of India, with its elitist concentration on higher education and massive neglect of basic health care, left that country poorly prepared for a widely shared economic expansion.[15]

China, by contrast,

> was not very far from the basic educational situation in South Korea or Taiwan, where too an educated population had played a major role in seizing the economic opportunities offered by a supportive market system.[16]

It is a sad reality that the past two decades of ANC rule have placed South Africa in the same league with India regarding social backwardness. This is why the masses of black South Africans are still waiting for the economic fruits of the transition to democracy. For these masses, the question is simple: where are the economic fruits of the transition? For how long must we continue to wait? Nobody knows.

Sterile economic ideas

It is not as though economic ideas were not entertained during the transition. The ANC's view was that economic challenges were not going to be addressed by markets alone, and thus the party initially expressed a preference for state intervention. An acknowledgement was also made that reliance on the state alone would be far from helpful. A commissioned report that was drawn up by the Macro-economic Research Group (MERG), comprising an eclectic mix of left-leaning academics and policy experts who had close links with trade unions and the ANC, made some proposals on how to restructure the economy. The substance of the proposals reflected a predisposition towards a state-driven approach within a social democratic framework.

Planned economic reforms for a new South Africa were managed as part of the negotiated settlement that characterised South Africa's transition from apartheid to democracy. Much of the negotiations over economic policy took place in secret. However, an attempt to legitimise the process was made through the establishment of a neo-corporatist mechanism called the National Economic Forum (NEF). This was to be a consensus-seeking instrument, consisting of ANC's economic mandarins, the trade union leadership, organised business and factions of the former National Party government. With the benefit of hindsight, and in the wake of the chaos that has engulfed the mining industry in recent times, questions have arisen regarding the effectiveness of the economic institutional arrangements agreed upon during the transition and how far-sighted these were.

During this period, the ANC developed the RDP with the intention to use it to guide its economic governance. It drew much from the earlier MERG report. From the outset, it emphasised the heritage of struggle to overcome institutional oppression and create the grand promise of a new South Africa. There were six principles that underpinned the RDP: an integrated and sustainable programme for development; a people-driven process; peace and security for all; nation-building; an inclusive growth approach; and democratisation of South Africa.[17] The social fractures that characterise our society today suggest that the ANC has not succeeded in bridging the gap between the loftiness of its promises and the actual conditions of the people of South Africa.

The RDP was too broad, playing to various constituencies and trying to strike a balance between disparate voices in an attempt to maintain the ANC's multi-class character. Even though it was genuine in its commitment to correcting social inequalities, the RDP failed to measure up as a serious programme for governance, nor was there any momentum generated by the ruling party to weave its strong social-democratic elements into a future policy programme. One of its severe limitations was the lack of a detailed implementation plan. The RDP office, which was established in 1996, located in Mandela's presidency, was eventually closed down, ostensibly due to its inability to allocate funds optimally. The main reason, though, was the confusion over its distinct role *vis-à-vis* other government departments.[18] Whatever the propaganda, what is incontrovertible is that the RDP failed to take off.

This is the fate that could well befall the currrent National Planning Commission, which is struggling to relate to a myriad of other economic policy functions of government which are diffused across the National Treasury, the Department of Trade and Industry and the Economic Development Department. The lack of focus and dwindling technical competencies may yet be a rerun of the failure of the RDP to take off. The black majority no longer have the patience they once possessed in the early days of transition.

It is now broadly accepted that there were a number of mistakes made in the initial phase of macro-economic reforms as part of the Gear framework, including over-reliance on sending signals to the international markets for attracting foreign direct investment.[19] The failure to develop a well-thought-out micro-economic strategy was another contributing factor. The hope that textbook trickle-down economics would be a magic bullet to overcome South Africa's deep-seated socio-economic challenges was blind faith of the highest order. It generated disappointment across the broad spectrum – from both left and right.

On the positive side, the Gear strategy did manage to ensure budget deficit reduction to levels aimed at by the government: below 3%. It improved predictability in monetary policy, and managed inflation and interest rate levels; and it created the basis for future social spending. The reality, however, is that the poor and unemployed are still waiting for the jobs once promised by Gear. When will they come? Again, nobody knows.

The most fundamental problem in the ANC's governing approach is that of severe institutional weaknesses. The highly unequal social structure of the past did not simply disappear at the moment of transfer of political power. Indeed, the large surplus of unskilled labour continued to increase after apartheid, with particularly low levels of labour market participation in rural areas.[20] The youth have been hit hard by unemployment. In a country that has 66% of its population under the age of 35, 71% of those aged between 24 and 35 are unemployed, and the majority of those people are black.[21]

The class advantages and disadvantages in the post-apartheid distributional regime continue to reproduce the race-based inequalities of the past. Without much direct support by the state and investment in education, those who are born in the townships and rural villages are least likely to make a transition to a better economic life, as they have to negotiate various hurdles and structural barriers to success. Their parents lack the assets to guarantee their economic success. The appalling condition of the education system presided over by the ANC makes it even more difficult for them to have a fighting chance in life.

Their counterparts in the white suburbs grow up in relatively better social conditions, surrounded by role models, and have a firmer socio-economic launching pad.

Ruchir Sharma observes:

The economic justice that was a chief promise of Mandela and the ANC remains a distant hope. Among blacks the rate of joblessness remains abnormally high (30%), but for whites it is markedly lower (6%) ... the income gap is just as wide today as it was when the ANC finally toppled the apartheid government nearly two decades ago.[22]

The top echelons of South Africa's managerial class are predominantly white, as is the ownership of the economy or physical assets in the form of titled home ownership. This is an indictment on the liberation movement that once promised economic emancipation to black people in South Africa.

Further, the traces of apartheid's social architecture remain deeply engraved in spatial planning, human settlement, differential educational standards and outcomes, economic exclusion, and race-based inequalities. In their social environments in the rural areas or townships, black youths see few role models who have pushed against barriers to success. Instead, most of them get absorbed into the informal economy, or into a life of economic inactivity.

These realities were not authored by the ANC as such; it is common cause that they are a legacy of apartheid. However, the ANC was brought to power with huge electoral support precisely to do away with these ills. In this it has failed dismally.

It is now clear that the early enthusiasm that characterised the transition from apartheid to democracy was largely informed by unrealistic expectations. While the country has made visible political progress, for the majority of black people this has yet to translate into tangible economic results. Driven by the lust for power, the ANC made economic promises it had no capacity to fulfil. The goalposts keep on shifting – from one election to the next. What does not shift in the minds of honest observers, though, is the reality that the ANC's economic policy experimentalism has been largely sterile.

Mythmaking, the lifeblood of the ANC

How did the ANC manage to dupe the people of South Africa? Since its years in exile, the ANC has assiduously cultivated an image of itself as a hero and a liberator. It portrayed itself as a people's liberation movement whose identity was tied to the aspirations of the black majority. It framed its purpose in the image of a saviour who would rescue South Africans from the grip of apartheid. That is how it won hearts and minds. Values such as non-racialism, non-sexism, human rights, and universal franchise put it in good standing in the eyes of the oppressed majority. This helped to earn the party favourable estimation both at home and abroad. All this was designed to induce a long-lasting feeling of indebtedness to the party among future generations of South Africans, especially the black majority. If you are black and critical of the ANC, you are easily branded a traitor, a counter-revolutionary and as furthering the objectives of 'liberals' – whatever this means. The image of the ANC as the ultimate saviour of black people immediately conjures up a massive wall beyond which it becomes almost impossible to conceive of other alternatives.

Although the ANC was banished into exile and had very limited contact with the South African people, it still managed to get its message across through propaganda such as Radio Freedom and its regular journal *Sechaba*. Instead of creating a gulf, the fact of exile fuelled the mystique of the ANC, and magnified the halo effect of a heroic liberator. So, although the ANC existed far away, the black majority thought of the organisation as part of their lives, and its ideology as a reflection of their aspirations.

Popular organisations such as the United Democratic Front (UDF), established in 1983, and civic organisations and trade unions that had been emboldened by the 1973 Durban strikes, did more to raise people's political consciousness and offered more organised resistance to apartheid than the ANC could have achieved in exile, yet the ANC was able to triumph ideologically as a vehicle for the expression of the aspirations of black people. It had what appeared to many as leadership depth because of towering characters such as Albert Luthuli, Oliver Tambo, Moses Kotane and many others.

The ANC further entrenched its myth as a people's liberator through songs, slogans, and symbols. It made one believe that its rudimentary military wing Umkhonto we Sizwe was well-equipped and could hold its own against the technically superior South African Defence Force. For the majority of South Africans, it was enough to know that there was a potentially powerful liberator who could walk across the border and deliver freedom for the people, and thus the people were in a mode of permanent expectation for such a moment to arrive. Their dreams about a better future were dreams about the return of the real leaders from exile to come and take over and deliver freedom. ANC songs were about this and they struck a deep chord in the emotions wearied by a ruthless apartheid system.

Yet very few South Africans knew the ANC intimately before it was unbanned. Many black people mostly assumed they knew the ANC through the slogans and cultural repertoire. Still, many today claim to know the ANC despite not having been part of it in exile or understanding the factors that shaped its character in the three decades it was under banishment.

To its credit, the ANC managed to fuse its political message with the aspirations of the people. The powerful hold of the ANC on the psyche of the black majority continued well into democracy. For a while after 1994, it was a rarity to find a black person who was critical of the ANC, except among remnants of the defunct homeland system. The party was elevated to the totem of liberation – a living ancestor of whom one dares not speak ill. Accordingly, the ANC could not under any circumstances be wrong. To probe the ANC's incompetence, post-apartheid, would be viewed by its leaders and supporters as an attack on the 'people', or as a 'counter-revolutionary' offensive. It still has not occurred to many people that the ANC is an ordinary political party, led by fallible individuals who are no different from a neighbour you might encounter in a shebeen. In many cases, your neighbour could do a far better job in government than many of our political elites in charge of the state are doing.

The ANC has an abundance of incompetents and, like any ordinary party, it is prone to failure. Even as it became clear that Jacob Zuma was a fundamentally flawed leader, few in society had the courage to acknowledge this fact, fearing the mythical might of the ANC. It is as if the party possesses ghostly powers, omnipotent and omnipresent, haunting every soul.

The very association of the ANC with the notion of 'the people' or 'the masses' inoculates it against public criticism. The Danish philosopher and cultural critic Søren Kierkegaard warns us against expressing fidelity to the abstract notion of the 'masses' (or 'the people'), but instead to insist on the truth. Believing the crowd as the court of last resort and as a legitimating force for political power induces a sense of powerlessness in the face of arrogant and unaccountable politicians.[23] What must not be forgotten is that the ANC is an ordinary party, populated by politicians who are susceptible to weaknesses, including weaknesses of the flesh: lust for power, corruption, greed, sexual exuberance, and all human follies.

It was therefore a collective failure of judgement for those who trusted the ANC too much to be the custodian of their future. They should have tempered their faith in a glorious future by insistence on accountability and the development of solid institutions that would stand as a citadel in defence of democracy when political leaders choose an abysmal path. Ours was a false optimism, a big political bubble to burst so badly in our own faces.

American business consultant and author Jim Collins illustrates the follies of false optimism through the personal account of US Admiral Jim Stockdale, the highest-serving US military officer in Vietnam's

'Hanoi Hilton' prisoner of war camp, who survived eight years in captivity. The paradox of the experience of the prisoners in the camp was that the optimists – those who always thought they would be freed from their captors the next Christmas – were outlived by those who were conscious of the brutal facts, and prepared to face them squarely.

Admiral Stockdale's take on his excruciating experience was: 'you must never confuse faith that you will prevail in the end … with the discipline to confront the most brutal facts of your current reality, whatever they might be'.[24] In the early years of our democracy, we pretty much buried our heads in the euphoric moment of change, and did not take care to consider the brutal realities that were to stare us frighteningly in the eye in years to come.

The early enthusiasm also blinded the ANC to future defects. The party did not pay sufficient attention to the important question of reproducing and sustaining strategic leadership beyond managing the transition from apartheid. There was absolutely no capacity to think beyond the now. Blinded by the larger-than-life image of Mandela, and the heroism of the ANC, the general citizenry was also complacent. The always necessary social task of developing leadership was outsourced to the ANC and the party that got hijacked by all manner of kleptocrats. Twenty years into democracy, the disastrous consequences for the rest of society are there for all to see, and all because society fell into the ANC's trap of mythmaking.

Our society fell into the trap by allowing the ANC to succeed in making citizens unwittingly buy into the party's philosophy of a big party and a small society. The predominant image is that the ANC is very powerful and that citizens are weak and therefore they can do nothing to force the party to be accountable. This is why when there are scandals involving senior people in government, it is as if the ANC does not care about the public. It is business as usual. No one resigns. The party is big, society is small. This is the danger of the ANC's mythmaking.

Abuse of history

In democratic South Africa, the ANC has continued to prop itself up through the invocation of history and selective memory to mask its massive governance failures. The British Marxist historian Eric Hobsbawm laments the politico-ideological abuse of history which reconstructs the substance of history to fit the particular biases of the present. A narrow invocation of history holds the danger of collapsing the sacred wall between fact and fiction. As Hobsbawm cautions: 'History as inspiration and ideology has a built-in tendency to become self-justifying myth. Nothing is a more dangerous blindfold than this ...'[25]

The point, though, is not to ignore the past or even to erase it from memory. What is dangerous is when history is deployed to blackmail future generations. The ANC is good at this. It uses history as the prism through which it views all of social life in contemporary South Africa. When in 2012 the ANC's provincial government in Limpopo failed to deliver textbooks to schools, Jacob Zuma blamed Hendrik Verwoerd. This is a classic case of history as a political instrument of blackmail. Verwoerd died on 6 September 1966, long before there was a province called Limpopo. Yet Zuma believes that, lying in his grave, Verwoerd had the ghostly powers to influence the distribution of textbooks in the year 2012 in Limpopo. Essentially, Zuma was using history to sustain the haunting image of a previous devil.

The blinding effect of the liberation mythology makes it difficult for many to contemplate political options beyond the ANC. They see its rule as decreed from above. This reinforces the sense of powerlessness in the face of the supposedly mighty and immortal ANC. This is what led most black voters to imagine a future ANC government as corruption-free or as a committee of priests. This false optimism made it appear as though all other parties were not fit to govern; or at least made it difficult to contemplate alternatives outside of the ANC.

The ANC continues to believe that its hold on power is unassailable.

It remains convinced that the black majority will always vote for it, no matter what. In its reasoning, the black voters are its captive political market, and they owe it an eternal debt for liberating them from apartheid. To further entrench its psychological hold, the ANC stigmatises anyone who professes sympathies for opposition parties as betraying the revolution. It is as if a black person has no individual conscience, or is not allowed to criticise the ANC. Voting for a different party is held up as a sin worse than infidelity. Yet the greatest freedom is the freedom to vote on the basis of conscience, to express individual power in relation to an external agency, and to make choices that are unburdened by other people's impositions.

This is the true meaning of political freedom.

The essence of all this is the construction of an ideology that makes people feel beholden to the ANC. In Marxist literature, where the notion of ideology has wider currency, it is often used to refer to the production of social meanings and beliefs to rationalise or reinforce the position of those whom are economically powerful.[26] The ANC has also thrived by producing meanings, beliefs, and signs (songs and slogans) that are intended to reinterpret history in a way that legitimates its political dominance post-apartheid. Memory, especially that of dispossession and institutionalised racism, is the backdrop the ANC has always used to reinforce its legitimacy. Prominent British literary critic Terry Eagleton states:

> A dominant power may legitimate itself by promoting beliefs and values congenial to it; naturalising and universalising such beliefs so as to render them self-evident and apparently inevitable; denigrating ideas which might challenge it; excluding rival forms of thought, perhaps by some unspoken systematic logic; and obscuring social reality in ways convenient to itself.[27]

Of course, the process of legitimation is not always asserted violently –

especially when a ruling party retains a firm grip on power on the back of mass support – but can be achieved by asserting its political hegemony through a rhetorical flourish that expresses the aspirations of the people, even though its actions may be incongruent with its rhetoric.

The ANC's conception of the National Democratic Revolution (NDR) was meant to solidify this rhetoric of struggle. The NDR forms a canvas onto which the ANC's historical myth may be projected. It offers an open-ended interpretation of the destination point of true liberation, allowing for the goalposts continually to be shifted along the way. This is a conception whose germination in the ANC was a result of the influence of the SACP during the exile years. It was then that the SACP managed to position itself as the intellectual vanguard of the liberation movement, subtly influencing the ANC's ideological character and shaping its practical programmes.

Accordingly, the NDR was an organising idea and conceptual framework of the steps to be taken towards the final defeat of apartheid. The dissolution of apartheid's institutional structures and the installation in power of an African nationalist party in the form of the ANC would be a significant landmark of such a struggle. It would pave the way for a socialist revolution, at the helm of which would be the SACP. All of this serves to entrench the myth of true freedom as realisable only via the ANC, however defective it has been at various stages of its life.

Where there are fundamental deficiencies of governance, they are airbrushed out as aberrations that will be fixed through a process of organisational renewal, and by refocusing energies towards building a developmental state. To be sure, the ANC's portrayal of itself, and that of South Africa, as on a permanent course of mending, is hardly new. In the exile years, at its weakest points it would formulate campaigns that were aimed to pull the wool over the eyes of its rank-and-file. For example, in the period between 1969 and 1974, the ANC launched what it called a 'Period of Regrouping and Recovery', followed in 1975 by another gimmick called 'The Period of Consolidation and Advance'.[28]

In the end, there was neither regrouping nor consolidation, but the rank-and-file spent valuable years running in circles, chasing fiction. When we hear the ANC today, howling gigantic platitudes or mouthing empty campaigns against corruption, when we can all see clearly that there is a glaring gap between word and the deeds of some of its members, we must remember that we are dealing with a political party which has, over the years, perfected the art of making people chase shadows.

The test of time

Twenty years after the first democratic elections, we stand at a vantage point. We see the early enthusiasm inspired by the boldness of F.W. de Klerk and the magnanimity of Nelson Mandela. The peace and political stability that we have enjoyed are indeed attributable to the leadership of these two individuals. Viewed from the vantage point of our time, it is perfectly understandable why the masses of oppressed black people listened to Mandela when he exhorted them to be patient. They anticipated the economic fruits that were to follow.

The vantage point of our time reveals a harsh reality, however; it is a reality of failed promises, of economic fruits that never came. It is a reality of mythmaking, intended to cloud the truth that the ANC government has failed to build effective public institutions that would help propel socio-economic progress in South Africa. There has been little recognition of the fact that, beyond personalities and the historical image of the ruling party, institutions are the best guardians of democracy. On this count we, the citizens, cannot entirely escape culpability; we have been complicit in allowing the ANC to destroy our society. The mythical character of the liberation movement and the abuse of history for political ends have lulled us into a socially suicidal slumber.

The story of South Africa's post-apartheid transition under the

leadership of the ANC is that of missed opportunities. The early idealism that accompanied the peaceful transition to democracy created
the illusion that the journey to political and economic Utopia would
be smooth and without hindrance or deviation. Time has proven that
ours has been a false optimism. As we march into the future, we must
learn from our past mistakes. We must never allow history again to be
subordinated to the political agendas of those in power. As Hobsbawm
reminds us, we have 'a responsibility to historical facts in general, and
for criticising the politico-ideological abuse of history in particular'.[28] If
we do not do this, the hope of rescuing history from political abuse will
remain what it currently is – a mere hope.

Chapter 4

HOW THE ANC IS FALLING

The success of political leaders ought to be measured by the extent to which their actions promote social and economic inclusiveness of their societies. The role of politicians should therefore be to advance the well-being of society, rather than self-enrichment. This kind of approach thrives better in democratic societies, where the normative framework of the political system is constructed around enhancing the capabilities of the citizens, as well as promoting the transparency and accountability of those who govern. This should not be construed to imply that such societies are without difficulties, or that they are devoid of incidents of corruption. It only means that there are clear frameworks, rules and institutions that discipline deviant behaviour whenever it occurs. Such nations generally succeed.

Inclusive societies are not difficult to describe. They are characterised by low levels of inequality, strong and effective public institutions, vibrant civil society formations, materially modest politicians, low levels of conspicuous consumption, and respect for and equality before the law. In such societies there are fewer scandals, and politicians embezzling public funds or caught up in all manner of sleaze are fairly rare. The political culture is that of personal responsibility, meaning that if you are found to have done something criminal, corrupt or morally indefensible, you fall. Scandinavian countries are not far from this description. In a climate like this, political parties have no choice but to adapt, or face the wrath of an unforgiving electorate. This is not heaven, far away from the irresistible temptations of earthly life.

Nations that fail, as American academics Daron Acemoğlu and James Robinson remind us, are those which are driven by an extractive motive, where institutions and individuals are all looking for opportunities to maximise selfish gain.[1] In the economy, in politics, in civil society, the first question is: what do I get from it? In such environments, political leaders behave like parasites, draining the resources of every possible victim – private or public.

In an extractive political system, the dominant mentality is that of the conman, ever perfecting ways and tricks to defraud people. Public institutions in such societies are appropriated and used as instruments of private accumulation by those who hold public office. If the prevailing political system is sham democracy – where citizens only matter on election day – swindlers master the art of hijacking political parties as vehicles of self-promotion. Once in office, they do what they are there to do – loot public money.

Standing in 2014, looking back over the past 20 years, has the ANC shown itself to be driven by an inclusive or extractive motive? The question is not whether the party has mouthed an inclusive agenda; it is whether the actual conduct of the party suggests a drift towards inclusivity or exclusivity. We say 'a drift towards' so as to answer the question: since 1994, has the ANC been moving from bad to worse, or the other way round?

Post-mortem results: Killed by factionalism

In its simplest definition, oligarchy means rule by the few. Applied to a country, it means that a small group of people determines the fate of the whole population. The same principle applies to an organisation;

an oligarchic core can take over a whole organisation. It is possible for a democratic country or organisation – with periodic elections – to be captured stealthily by an oligarchy. In other words, a small group of members of a political party can plot the outcomes of an election by using underhand dealings to influence them.

Vote buying, factionalism, tribalism and cabalism are some of the methods used by oligarchs to control organisations, and ultimately societies. These instruments are often difficult to verify because, by their very nature, they are clandestine. No one wants to be caught buying votes, few people want it known that they are leaders of a faction, no one advertises himself as a cabalist, and few people confess to being tribalists. Yet all of these phenomena do exist. They are practices done by real human beings, in real organisations.

Oligarchs are associated with exclusivity, not inclusivity. Members of an oligarchy generally view themselves as special, a chosen group that must determine who gets what in a political system. They can decide to include certain members of a different group for self-determined purposes, and they can exclude whomever they deem deserving of exclusion. Inclusive societies or organisations cannot be built on oligarchies, for, unlike rules-based systems, oligarchies cannot be predicted. They are as fickle as they are whimsical.

Before the 2007 Polokwane conference of the ANC, South Africans had been fed the well-cooked propaganda of a cohesive, united and faction-free ANC. The heroism that attached to the ANC as a liberation movement in the early years of democracy in South Africa had numbed observers into accepting uncritically the products of party spin-doctoring. The mythical personality of Nelson Mandela did not leave room for people to subject ANC mythology to critical scrutiny. The only side people were prepared to see was the one decorated with stories of liberation struggle gallantry. Anyone who dared question the party of Mandela was on the wrong side of liberation morality, and thus regarded as one with former oppressors – white racists. Cloaked by the heroic personality of Mandela, the ANC strutted about like an untouchable moral giant, wearing boots so heavy they could flatten every irritating ant. The sanctimonious, ever-present image of Mandela cast a shadow of righteousness upon his political party.

All this came to a dramatic end in 2007, when the party was torn into two unforgiving factions – one led by Thabo Mbeki and the other by Jacob Zuma. The intensity of factional hatred was so deep that all previous pretensions of unity dropped their masks. The drama was performed on an open stage for all to see. This is how the domineering Mbeki was kicked out of the leadership of the ANC, and how the motley, sticky-fingered Zuma-supporting crew shot to power.

To a reader who has accepted the cynical view of factionalism as the essential motor that propels politics, the deeper, exclusionist implications of factional politics may not immediately reveal themselves. This was the case in the tussle between Mbeki and Zuma supporters. To such a reader, this tussle, back in 2007, may have appeared like an internal party affair that had little to do with the South African population. But, hardly a year after Polokwane, the Zuma supporters subjected the whole country to utterly unnecessary political instability by deploying gangster-like tactics to overthrow Mbeki and evict him from the Union Buildings. When this happened, the rest of the world watched in disbelief as South Africa was reduced to a political circus, and the sharpened claws of party factional fighters did not spare innocent South Africans any scars.

It was a period of great political trauma for a young nation whose soul had hardly taken shape. When Mbeki was removed from government, the ANC was torn into two camps: one was filled with vindictive triumphalists who could not wait to take up financially rewarding positions in government, while the other was populated with soul-battered mourners who could not imagine life after power. Some among the latter broke out and formed the Congress of the People (COPE), a short-lived political party which succumbed to the very cancer that was busy killing the ANC: factionalism.

The biggest lesson to be learnt from COPE is simple: out of rot comes rot. Any party formed by former ANC members seems to carry cancerous factional cells long before it is born. This is a genetic condition acquired during gestation in the womb of its dying mother, the ANC. South Africans who celebrated the birth of COPE did so because they did not understand how the ANC passes factional diseases from its poisoned bloodstream to the offspring who later disavow their parents. No sooner had COPE supporters finished celebrating the birth of the new baby when the promising child began to show signs that it had inherited all the fatal ailments of its mother. The mood of COPE supporters swung rapidly from celebration to grief. There was a sense of betrayal – a feeling akin to that experienced by mourners who gather to bury the body of someone who has died very young.

The political road to the Polokwane conference revealed just how perverted the ANC's system of internal 'democracy' is. The true character of the party, that of an oligarchic ensemble controlled by cliques that develop candidate lists and manipulate the way branches vote, was laid bare. Polokwane marked the beginning of the reign of slates, and this continued well into the party's 2012 national conference in Mangaung. In a slate democracy, such as that of the ANC, voters are treated like automated machines, programmed never to deviate from the instructions of the oligarchs who determine lists long before elective conferences. If this is democracy, it is sham democracy.

As the ANC has been dominating South Africa over the past 20 years and, given the country's system of proportional representation, it was inevitable that what has been happening electorally inside the party would also be imposed upon the whole country. The ANC's electoral conferences have been the real locus of the country's political power. Once a person is elected party president, in a sham democracy that person is assured of becoming the country's head of state. In this situation, the nocturnal oligarchs who controlled the ANC also had power over the country as a whole. This is why the battle for positions in the party became a matter of life and death, with party members literally killing each other in order to preside over state patronage. On the eve of the Mangaung conference, in December 2012, Obuti Chika, the then regional secretary of the Kenneth Kaunda district, was murdered in the North West province. His former comrade China Dodovu – who was then MEC for local government and traditional affairs – was arrested for this crime and charged with murder and conspiracy to commit murder, although the case was still ongoing at the time of publication. This is what our country has been reduced to, by a party – the ANC, to which most South Africans once entrusted all their aspirations. It is the same party as the one Nelson Mandela led into democracy.

The problem with factional battles is that they are a zero-sum game: the battles are ruthless; they aim at obliterating. Either members of this faction are in charge or else members of another faction are in charge. There is no middle ground. Since members of factions are conscious of this brutal necessity, they fight with the determination of a ferocious destroyer. The principle is clear: if you do not destroy, you will be destroyed. The purging of pro-Mbeki factionalists, following the dethronement of their political principal post-Polokwane, was a manifestation of this ruthless principle.

Ordinary South Africans wouldn't care less if this factionalism was confined to the ANC, but the reality is that it does spill over into the realm of the state. When factions within the party pursue each other, they do not stop simply because whoever they are pursuing occupies a position in government. In any case, the ultimate end of factional battles is to capture state power. The objective is to have access to state resources as an instrument of political patronage. Thus we cannot say that the South African public is insulated from the ANC's factional wars. Ordinary South Africans are innocent victims of these bitter wars and when the ANC is finally declared dead, the factional poison of its carcass will not leave society intact.

Corruption, the new emblem of the ANC?

Corruption ranks very high among the afflictions that have deformed the face of the ANC. Given the high-sounding principles mouthed by so-called cadres of the party – principles of selflessness and dedication to the poor, among others – the rapaciousness witnessed amongst members of the ANC is hard to believe. Reflecting on corruption in the Communist Party of China under Mao Zedong, Chinese human rights activist Liu Xiaobo was troubled by the question: 'How do vanguards, who are supposed to be well-disciplined and deployable, become corrupt?'[2] With regard to the ANC, this question is equally troubling.

What makes corruption difficult to deal with is that when it takes over an institution – a political party, a government entity, a private firm, a church, an NGO – it does not stand by the door and announce its arrival: 'Hello, my name is Corruption. I am here.' If this were the case, those inside would reply, 'No, don't come in. You are not welcome.' By the same token, organisations never convene a gathering to pass a resolution to become corrupt. But they do adopt positions against corruption.

Corruption generally worms its way into organisations through members who are already inside, members who are counted amongst the most loyal and trusted cadres. It is for this reason that when allegations of corruption surface against a trusted member, the first reaction by the general membership is that of disbelief and denial.

This was the case when Tony Yengeni, who enjoyed a cult status among cadres in parts of the Western Cape, and who became the ANC's chief whip under Thabo Mbeki, was arrested for corruption in October 2001.

The Yengeni case revealed serious weaknesses in the character of the ANC. For the first time since 1994, it became clear that while some in the leadership of the organisation may have been serious about corruption, there were many who did not believe that it was fair to punish fellow comrades who were convicted of corruption. When Yengeni was sentenced to imprisonment, he was hoisted on the shoulders of a group of exuberant comrades, who chanted and sang struggle songs, suggesting that their comrade had been treated unfairly. Our supposedly virtuous ANC cadres, some of whom were prominent leaders, were effectively giving the judiciary the middle finger. It was the kind of political sympathy that revealed that the ANC was synonymous with corruption.

Strikingly, the leadership of the ANC did not issue a statement condemning those who gave Yengeni a hero's send-off to prison. Not a single one of these sympathisers was hauled before the party's disciplinary committee. For the public, the message was loud and clear: if you are a member of the ANC, you will always be supported, however corrupt you may be.

This message was confirmed years later, in 2007, when the 52nd National Conference of the ANC elevated Yengeni to the coveted status of being a member of its National Executive Committee (NEC) to head its political education – presumably to spread the party's morality to the rest of its flock. Members of the party did this knowing full well that Yengeni was a convicted fraudster. When this was done, the perception of the ANC as a party which endorses corruption was confirmed as reality. This was an actual case of someone who had been found guilty of corruption being rewarded with a senior position of leadership. It was as if to say, 'We are very sorry, comrade Yengeni, that you served time in prison. Please accept a position on the NEC as a token of our remorse.'

What the ANC may not have realised was that by rewarding a convicted criminal, Yengeni, it was promoting corruption as an element of the organisation's political culture, and that other criminals would be inspired by the case of Yengeni, and as a result view the ANC as a safe home for convicted criminals. What was profane had been promoted as the new creed of morality in the ANC. How could the ANC, in future, prevent people with criminal records from occupying positions of leadership in the organisation? More importantly, how would the party serve as a role model for good behaviour in society?

At its Polokwane national conference in 2007, the ANC demonstrated that it did not care about these ethical questions. The party promoted Jacob Zuma to the top position of president. Two years later, in 2009, he became state president. Zuma's misdemeanours are well known. When he was elected president of the ANC, he had more than 700 criminal cases – including corruption – hanging over his head. The charges were dropped by the NPA, which meant that not one of these cases was dismissed by a court of law. These cases disappeared into a fog through political machinations involving National Intelligence, out of which they have yet to emerge. This is how Zuma's path was paved to the Union Buildings.

Had this not been done, Zuma could possibly be mingling with very dangerous criminals in one of South Africa's maximum security prisons. To this day, and despite charges being dropped, a cloud hangs over Zuma's head. As president of the ANC, he personally has cast a dark shadow of corruption upon his party. With Zuma at the top, the ANC keeps the acronym but has acquired an unenviable image and different wording: Alleged National Criminal organisation.

There are those who believe that it is only a few rotten apples that are problematic in the ANC. Such people think that like a river casting away aberrant elements, the ANC will cleanse itself of impurities. The reality, though, is that there aren't just a few rotten apples; corruption has become endemic in the ANC and so the party cannot cleanse itself without first committing suicide. It must die first before it can have any hope of resurrecting itself with a new, purified soul.

There are members of the party who view the ANC as a ticket to instantaneous prosperity. The problem is that, once such members are seen to succeed, their practices become generalised as the new culture of the organisation. As Patrick Chabal and Jean-Pascal Daloz point out in *Africa Works*, corruption is not

> *a matter of a few 'rotten apples' or of a venal 'class', even less an evil to be eradicated by means of vigorously 'ethical' campaigns. On the contrary, it is a habitual part of everyday life, an expected element of every social transaction.*[3]

In this context, to be an ANC member is to have one foot in the door of patronage, depending on whether one is aligned to a powerful oligarch at branch, regional, provincial or national level. Thus to be a leader is to be in a position to influence procurement contracts at these levels of government.

The post-1994 environment of access to state power has caused the ANC to lose its sense of historic mission. Today it is hard to discern the party's animating mission beyond hollow slogans, unaccompanied by practical action by the party's leadership and members. While there are a few leaders with integrity, they are overwhelmed by the never-ending scandals of corruption: from the Arms Deal to Travelgate, from Guptagate to Nkandlagate. Soon the ANC's murky river will spit its few untainted cadres out, just like the French Revolution became a monstrosity, sending to the guillotine some of its architects, including its finest minds.

At its national conference in December 2012, the ANC established an 'integrity commission', ostensibly to cleanse the party of corrupt elements. At the same time, the party elected to its highest decision-making body people who had been implicated in the abuse of state resources, such as Humphrey Memezi, former Gauteng MEC responsible for local government. The conference also returned Jacob Zuma to the presidency of the party, despite fresh allegations of more than R206 million of public money being spent to give his private compound in Nkandla a facelift. By doing this, the ANC unwittingly rendered its decision to establish an integrity commission a joke. It is either wilful gullibility or naivety of the worst order that would attach a modicum of seriousness to the ANC's integrity commission.

There are multifarious reasons why the ANC appears tolerant of corruption. Among these is the attitude that party cadres who were in exile spent the time they could have used to advance themselves materially fighting for liberation. Barry Gilder, a liberation struggle veteran of the ANC, was honest in representing those who harbour this feeling. Here is what he said:

> Those of us who came out of struggle or deprivation into the private sector, assailed by the same temptations, seemed to have no choice but to play economic and lifestyle catch-up through the only advantage we had – our special, political, and struggle network.[4]

For Gilder and his comrades, the quickest catch-up path has been through government positions, state procurement systems or BEE. As players who bore the powerful stamp of ANC approval, the comrades were indeed better placed, but it is a mentality of righteous victimhood, an attitude that conceals venality behind political correctness.

This kind of mentality attaches no importance to agency, that is, the ability of individuals to choose between right and wrong, when confronted with ethical questions in life. There are individuals within the ANC who also made personal sacrifices under apartheid, but chose not to participate in shady deals post-apartheid. They have their principles to live and die for. These are not people made of saintly stuff, but people who had a more enduring motive and a sense of meaning that projected beyond personal comfort and instant gratification. These individuals could not sacrifice their souls at the altar of materialism.

We make this point to dispel the myth that seeks to justify corruption as some kind of political necessity for ANC cadres who lost time in the liberation struggle. This manufactured necessity is self-serving. It is a myth that is as dehumanising as it is kleptocratic. Losing time in the liberation struggle cannot justify the death of conscience. It cannot be that those who were in the struggle returned to normal life with a twisted sense of humanity.

We must thank Barry Gilder, though – he was honest enough publicly to shed light on the dark side of the ANC's character. Very few among ANC veterans are as honest as Gilder. But there is a gap in his rationalisation. His is a rear-view mirror perspective. It tells us little about younger ANC leaders, who were never in exile or prison, leaders who are alleged to be corrupt without the 'excuse'. Julius Malema, an expelled ANC Youth League firebrand owed the South African Revenue Services (SARS) more than R16 million by the time he was expelled from the ANC. He had property worth millions – expensive mansions, farms and a loaded trust account. By the time Malema was expelled, he was only 30 years old, and had never held a formal job in his life, other than being a young politician in the ANC. Before Malema, Fikile Mbalula also presided over an ANC Youth League whose leaders allegedly were made filthy rich by the slain corrupt tycoon, Brett Kebble. Where did these young leaders waste their time? They were not in exile, but they also played their own version of catch-up.

It would be interesting to hear Gilder's rationalisation of the enrichment of young ANC leaders. What seems clear, though, is that the young are good at learning from the old. As Gilder and his generation were busy playing catch-up, the young ones were observing and learning. In other words, it is the old who passed the baton of economic entitlement on to the younger generation. This is why it is impossible to rescue the ANC; its younger leaders are arguably as corrupt as some of their elders. They are thoroughly socialised into a morality authored in the chambers of hell. There is a continuity of evil in the corrupted political culture of the ANC. Corruption is like an inherited disease – passed on through the genes of the father to the son.

The view that the ANC is being corrupted from outside has its own believers. Former ANC member of parliament Andrew Feinstein suggests that corruption cannot be understood separately from external factors such as the workings of global capitalism. He uses the example of the infamous South African Arms Deal to make the point that ANC officials were sucked into an existing network of corruption in the global arms industry.[5] Heribert Adam, Van Zyl Slabbert and Kogila Moodley place part of the blame for the rise of corruption on foreign governments and donors who dispensed funding to parties without insisting on accountability to the public.[6] Whatever the causes, none of these authors claims that there is no corruption in the ANC.

Even high-ranking officials in the ANC have decried the state of corruption in the party. In his organisational report, delivered to the party's National General Council in 2010, Gwede Mantashe lamented the rise of ill-discipline, infighting and the influence of money in party structures. The political damage done by these ills has been noted repeatedly by other leaders at lower levels of the party. In 2011, for example, David Makhura's soul was tormented by the ills afflicting the ANC:

> *Given the destructive tendencies that have crept into the fabric of our organisation, all of us must be worried that the centenary should not represent the last highpoint in the glorious history of the ANC.*[7]

Makhura spoke like a prophet, haunted by a vision of a future without his organisation – the ANC. He agonised like a son fully cognisant that his cancerous mother is about to depart, forever.

As with factionalism, corruption by ANC leaders does affect ordinary citizens. It drains resources that were intended to improve the lives of the poor and vulnerable in society. The more than R206 million spent on Jacob Zuma's private compound in Nkandla could have gone a long way in making the lives of the poor better: children who spend wintry nights in shacks could be sleeping in warm, brick-and-mortar houses; those without water could be drinking clean water for the first time in their lives.

In March 2013, the auditor-general noted that R24.8 billion was wasted in unauthorised, irregular, and fruitless expenditure by provincial governments. The South African Institute of Race Relations estimated that this amount could have paid for child support grants for 7.4 million children; it could have built more than 400 schools and could have improved the country's water and sanitation infrastructure.[8]

The corruption within the ranks of the ANC also has a negative impact on the image of the country as a whole. Two decades since the end of apartheid, South Africa's profile as a country tolerant of corruption has worsened. In 2010 South Africa was ranked 54 out of 183 countries on Transparency International's Corruption Perception Index (1 is the cleanest and 183 the most corrupt). A year later (in 2011), South Africa lost 10 positions, falling to 64; in 2012, it dropped to 69; and in 2013 it lost a further three places – to 72. This means that, since 2010, South Africa has become more corrupt and, as we write this book, there are no signs that this tide is about to be reversed.

Corruption in the ranks of the ANC cannot be explained on the basis of apartheid, as those in the ANC are wont to believe. Nor can it be rationalised on the basis of the existence of a corrupt 'capitalist' network, as Barry Gilder and others would have us believe. The ANC was fighting apartheid, and it would make better sense for us to expect members of the party to be *less* corruptible compared to the apartheid state. Also, the ANC's is not the only government in the world operating under capitalist economic conditions. Using apartheid and capitalism as excuses is absolute baloney. As Van Zyl Slabbert points out: 'It is possible to do honest business.'[9] That the ANC itself appears to have no interest in doing honest business is best exemplified by the existence of Chancellor House, the party's investment vehicle, which is effectively a front organisation making money by hook or crook for the party.

Access to economic resources through state power has had a fatal effect on the lofty brand of the ANC. When we suggest the fall of the ANC, we mean that in popular psychology the redemptive image of the party has withered away due to the widespread venality within its ranks. It has gotten to the point where ordinary South Africans draw a distinction between Nelson Mandela and the ANC they see today.

Mandela is generally understood to represent a different ANC, the ANC before the fall of the party. The ANC after the fall is a party of ordinariness, stripped of the extraordinariness of Oliver Tambo and his generation, or at least those who were not corrupted by access to state resources. The ANC of today makes observers wonder: what does this mean for the future of South Africa? Posed differently, the question is: after the fall of the ANC – what next?

Exile, where the rot began

Where did all this begin? Much of the ANC's history in exile is couched in mythology. The party's propagandists would be very happy for posterity to believe the myth of a righteous party, populated by human angels, harmoniously drinking milk and honey in exile. As we have already observed, this image is a lie the cadres feed on. The ANC is simply perpetuating what Eric Hobsbawm calls the politico-ideological abuse of history. This abuse finds expression in the reconstruction of history to perpetuate the myth that the liberation movement possessed messianic properties, and fought a heroic battle, unsullied by acts of corruption.

There is a view that in the ANC's liberation struggle there were no abuses, apart from negligible aberrations in some camps in exile. If we believe this piece of historical revisionism, the contemporary character of the ANC as, in our opinion, a corrupt organisation, or as an Alleged National Criminal organisation, would not make sense. Nobody must fall into this trap. In his most recent work, *External Mission*, a study of the ANC's existence in exile from the early 1960s to the early 1990s, Stephen Ellis recounts incidents of ill-discipline, factionalism and corruption in the top command of various ANC MK camps. This was a period when the ANC existed largely outside of the country after it was banned in 1960. It was a period of turmoil, a chapter in human history that sane people wouldn't like to see reopened.

The only known facts about the ANC in exile were through propaganda channels designed to fit the preferred script of the party's leadership, to portray the party as being in good health. Very few people would know about the compromising activities of the ANC in exile. Many deliberately don't want to know the truth because it would hurt too much or call into question their own identity, an identity constructed out of an image of the party, an image embellished with ideological dogma and propaganda that might be false. Because ordinary black South Africans were yearning for heroes, they were prone to believe the ANC's version of truth – truth according to the party. At the time, it was blasphemous to take a critical stand against the ANC because it was regarded widely as a legitimate vehicle to carry the aspirations of the black majority. Tactically, this was good for the ANC.

It did not matter that people were far from the ANC's real experience in exile, and that they did not really know its leaders. Sentiment alone was sufficient to create the connection. They felt a part of the ANC's world. Its rhetoric appealed to them. The organisation's existence in exile was in their name. Living under apartheid, ruled by the most vicious government, examining the ANC's deficiencies under a microscope would have been inconceivable and extremely difficult to do anyway. Much of this history is superbly summarised by the works of Vladimir Shubin, who offers a sympathetic account,[10] and Stephen Ellis, who offers a dispassionate reflection.[11]

Corruption and factionalism have a much deeper lineage in the ANC than is sometimes acknowledged. In *External Mission*, Ellis details deeply entrenched factional tensions in the ANC's exile missions,

promotion of cadres on grounds of loyalty rather than on merit, existence of corruption, and the tenuous leadership of Oliver Tambo, who
preferred to avoid conflict by establishing special committees of inquiry
to tackle problems in MK camp life. These would yield no satisfacto-
ry outcome, but would magnify the image of Tambo as a reconciler
and consummate diplomat. Yet the problems would continue to fester
beneath the surface, and Tambo would be long gone, hoisting his pro-
verbial trophy as a reconciler of note.

The reality was that the ANC in exile was a disparate organisation,
engaged in internecine factional battles. It had an uneasy relationship
with the SACP, and it was bedevilled by ill-discipline amongst its cadres. According to Ellis, tensions between groups would sometimes take
on a 'worrying ethnic dimension', at times escalating to confrontations
amongst the rank-and-file within MK. Factional manoeuvres and the
building of close-knit circles of loyalists were some of the ANC's hall-
marks in exile. As Ellis further observes, this virus included financial
corruption, illicit car trade, and drug smuggling and illicit diamond
dealings becoming commonplace in some camps.[12] This was not just
amongst the ordinary members of MK; it was a practice in which some
in the leadership participated.

This state of affairs prompted the ANC's national working committee to establish a sub-committee in September 1980 specifically to look
into corruption. Inertia was the best survival mechanism. After all,
there was a much bigger enemy to battle with than to raise controversy
about the conduct of the leadership in exile. The ANC being steeped in
African nationalism as an embodiment of the struggle of the oppressed
African masses made it difficult for blacks to be critical of it without
coming across as betraying a grand struggle and working to promote
the counter-revolutionary objectives of the enemy.

Those who had raised their voice against the leadership in exile were
either thrown into jail, as was the case with Chris Hani and his group
when they criticised poor leadership in the wake of the failed Wankie

Campaign in 1968, or the 'Gang of Eight' which was expelled in the 1970s for being critical and exhibiting ideological discordance. In some instances, the very same tactics used by the National Party security forces against freedom fighters would be deployed by the ANC against its own operatives if it suspected them of misdeeds.

As it ascended to power, the ANC never took time to reflect on the likely impact of its dirty past on the character of the party going forward. It never had a moment of reflection on its time in exile, the excesses that were committed during this period, and the corrupt practices that became a part of its lifeblood. The failure to do so and the predisposition to defend the leadership at all costs has become the bane of the ANC today. Without understanding the ANC's rot in exile, it would be impossible to trace the seeds of its degeneracy in our time.

A mafia state in the making

There is a rise of transactional leadership on the back of the growing corruption and factionalism within the ANC. The unseemly bonds between the ruling party and factions of business post-apartheid bear a striking resemblance in our view to the mafia state that evolved in post-communist Russia under Boris Yeltsin. Stark parallels include preference by the ruling party for acquiescent business elite who are in search of tickets to prosperity. A transactional leadership is a central feature of this reality. In a transactional leadership, the relations between the state and business are not based on a shared vision about a better future, but in order to share the spoils of patronage.

In his book, *Endgame*, Willie Esterhuyse cautions against transactional leadership:

> *It is self-evident that transactional leadership opens the door to corruption and promotes the possibility of opportunistic compromises.*

It is transactional leaders that convert fragile states and uncertain democracies into criminal states.[13]

In both countries, access to state-sanctioned commercial opportunities is given to a few elites in exchange for their loyalty to the ruling party. In return, they are guaranteed commercial prosperity. Because of their close proximity to the ruling party, these businessmen are expected to overlook institutional failures of the state.

In the current environment, this means more than just loyalty to the party, but willingness to safeguard the material welfare of its leaders and family members. The hideous umbilical cord between the ruling party and factions of business was exposed recently in President Jacob Zuma's admonition to business during an ANC's anniversary gala dinner: 'I have always said that a wise businessman will support the ANC, because supporting the ANC means you're investing very well in your business.'[14] He might as well have added: 'If you go a step further to support me and my family, you will reap a richer harvest.'

In Russia, especially after Yeltsin's second term in office from July 1996, there was a coterie of highly influential and self-serving businessmen whose success was aided by the chaotic privatisation programme that bankrupted the state and stifled genuine entrepreneurship. At the same time, many Russians became poorer and the country's infrastructure was fast collapsing.

Russia's oligarchs had no interest in contributing to the renewal of the nation's spirit or in the economic welfare of the citizens who had suffered many decades of devastation under communist rule. These elites possessed no shared social purpose, apart from enriching themselves. Oligarchs such as Anatoly Chubais, the then chairman of the agency responsible for privatisation, witnessed instantaneous change in fortunes; they amassed wealth at the expense of the country's economic stability.[15] Despite being implicated in sleazy deals, Chubais was handsomely rewarded with a cushy position as Yeltsin's chief-of-staff, thereby giving him access to vast political influence, which he used to augment his wealth further.

Many other oligarchs prospered through a web of lucrative commercial interests in media, real estate and natural resources. Some, such as Boris Berezovsky, once a leading media mogul in the country, also enjoyed the favoured status of being part of Yeltsin's inner family circle. His political proximity landed him an influential position in Russia's security council. Yeltsin's weakness as a leader made him a menace to the nation's security. His smile and affability belied a vicious core.

In her book, *Sale of the Century,* Chrystia Freeland paints a picture of Yeltsin in the words of one of the oligarchs:

> *He is an interesting personality – dangerous, but interesting. He is like a bear: he seems always to have such a good-natured smile, but it is known that the bear is the most dangerous beast for its trainers.*[16]

Indeed, Yeltsin sold his country's precious jewels to a coterie of robber capitalists, and allowed it to sink deeper into misery. Consideration of his personal survival trumped everything else.

Zuma is Yeltsin incarnate. His presidency signals a security threat for the country – economic and political. South Africa's equivalents of Russia's oligarchs are men of influence such as members of the Gupta family. They represent a tiny but growing layer of business elite whose informal power reaches to the highest echelons of the state, allegedly extending influence on just about everything – from the conduct of the police force to the deployment of associates to state-owned entities. Their choreographed public image is at odds with their conduct and their deeply ingrained sense of entitlement.

The danger for society is that these incestuous bonds breed cynicism. They open up the state to corrupt influences of businessmen with no interest in the vitality of the country. In this culture, other corporates will lose the will to champion progressive economic change and

South Africa could find itself becoming a mafia state in the mould of Yeltsin's Russia. But, then, the ANC cares little about public opinion. It lives under the illusion that the majority of South Africans will continue to vote for it no matter what. It views itself as occupying an unassailable position in the psyche of the black majority, and so it continues to ride the crest of the wave of its fading historical glory and symbols. It is the notion that the ANC is a benefactor that brought liberation that deepens its arrogance.

Hero-worshipping amongst the majority of the population makes it harder to hold elites accountable. Leaders are seen to possess a monopoly on wisdom and are thereby over-celebrated. Political leaders, especially ministers, lack humility and are possessed of an inflated sense of grandeur. The notion that they are servants is completely foreign to them. Amongst politicians it is often forgotten that the Latin root meaning for the word 'minister', simply stated, is servant or attendant. In South Africa, it has prima donna connotations. To question a minister who is involved in some act of corruption, or who has committed an irregularity, is viewed by those in power as a sign of disrespect. It hardly occurs to them that by their actions they disrespect the public.

It is the two dangerous forces of corruption and factionalism that are hastening the ANC's demise. This hideous image of the party as tolerant of corruption and faction-ridden might have its origins in the early years of democracy but this has worsened under Jacob Zuma. When the ANC came to power in 1994, amidst the euphoria that accompanied its ascendance, the party did not imagine that its support base could one day erode, with the real possibility of losing power. While this may not happen in a Big Bang fashion, trends since the 2009 elections suggest a downward spiral. The reality is that, on the African continent, liberation movements that go down never rise again. The ANC is unlikely to regain the electoral losses it is incrementally making.

As *Financial Times* news editor Alec Russell points out:

> As the ANC settled into government in April 1994, its leaders bridled
> when commentators compared their beloved party to other liberation
> movements or even predicted they too might lose their way.[17]

Today the ANC's loss of moral compass is commonplace. It is a new
normality that the party faithful would want us to adjust to. The ANC's
leadership bench is becoming thinner as the dough of corruption rises.
The political culture of the party and the character of its leadership go
a long way to explaining the morass the country finds itself in today.

In the era of Nelson Mandela, it was difficult sharply to point to incidents of corruption, yet spaces for these were widening even then. The
massive Arms Deal happened on Mandela's watch. He was president
at the time. This dodgy arms procurement and the corruption that
underpinned it has now become public knowledge, and has revealed
the extent of the corruptibility of some leading figures within the ANC.

The view of leaders as heroes has helped to facilitate the growth of
corruption and its terrifying continuity under Jacob Zuma. There is no
sign that this will abate any time soon. In fact, we contend that the idea
of Zuma serving another term as president of South Africa raises the
spectre of a mafia state *à la* Russia under Boris Yeltsin.

Society, be vigilant

The damage of the ANC's political hegemony is that it has wrought
destruction on the nascent trust that was under construction in the
early years of democracy. It has also weakened the legitimacy of public
leadership in the eyes of society, even of those who might well be clean
and committed to good governance. The cynicism that the ANC's poor
political leadership has bred has torn asunder the framework of trust

between citizens and public leadership. When virtues of governance are no longer seen in a favourable light, it is much more difficult for citizens to trust any politician or public authority figure.

When there is no trust between those who hold political office and the country's citizens, the legitimacy of those who govern becomes shallow. Trust is a soft infrastructure which helps to solidify the threads that hold society together and form the pillar to which institutions that regulate political behaviour are anchored. American political scientist Francis Fukuyama suggests that high-trust societies tend to have higher institutional reliability as opposed to low-trust societies which are marked by corruption and high administrative costs. Indeed, as he points out, trust helps to create certainty in how individuals and institutions function.[18]

The disintegration of trust in societies often begins with the failure of integrity in public leadership. Transitional societies such as South Africa need more, not less, integrity from their political leaders. Trust is the most critical capital that helps sustain progress. In transitional societies, institutional foundations which regulate political behaviour and guarantee accountability tend to be fragile, which is why trust is important to such societies.

Advanced countries that have had time to create and entrench solid institutions depend less on individual politicians to facilitate social progress. In such cases, institutions have an independent agency power and contain in-built disciplinary mechanisms that are triggered when politicians act contrary to acceptable norms. This is why Austro-British philosopher Karl Popper declared the following as the most important question of politics: 'How can we organise political institutions so that bad or incompetent rulers can be prevented from doing too much damage?'[19] The fragility of institutions in transitional societies means that political leaders, depending on whether they are transactional or transformational leaders, could make or break their societies. This is why South Africans must be vigilant.

Generally, institutions that mediate the relationship between leaders and citizens are founded on a social contract that has both formal and informal constraints designed to limit the excesses of public office holders. Formal constraints would, for example, be in the form of independent agencies that act decisively against acts of corruption. These constraining mechanisms would assume the form of a transparent and enforceable sets of rules that circumscribe or prescribe behaviour on the part of those who hold public office.

Informal constraints are expressed in the shape of certain codes of conduct, norms of behaviour, and conventions about what is acceptable and not acceptable. These may not necessarily be written down, but it would be assumed that those who hold public office are motivated, for example, by a sense of honour, and that their motivation is primarily to improve the quality of public institutions, and therefore that of citizens. Together these constraints, formal and informal, constitute a significant part of what is referred to as political culture, or the character of a nation's politics.

The power of informal constraints means that if wrongdoing is detected, politicians do not wait for commissions of inquiry, but act honourably and resign from their positions. At the point at which trust between them and citizens is compromised, their ability to enhance the ethical value of institutions comes under question. Their legitimacy, too, comes under a critical spotlight. Accordingly, public trust and substantive legitimacy is more important than their egos. For example, when it is suspected that someone who holds public office has knowingly deceived the public regarding the use of public funds, as was the case in Nkandlagate, it should not be necessary to wait for a formal investigation to reveal this. A sense of honour should dictate resignation. The implications for non-action are that the formal institutions which have to be deployed to investigate the many misdemeanours of the president become weakened.

Such a political culture is all but impossible to establish under the

ANC's rule. The party has drowned deep in allegations of corruption, and has a wrong-headed view of its power relations with the rest of society. It has lost the capacity to construct a framework for a high-trust society. Believing that the ANC can establish such a framework is not different from entrusting serial criminals with the honourable responsibility of developing a penal code.

As Robert Rotberg, a frequent commentator on conflict in the developing world, reminds us: 'without legitimacy, effective government is impossible'.[20] It is trust-based legitimacy that lends authority its source of power. Currently, the governing party does not enjoy substantive legitimacy because there has been a failure of trust, occasioned by the many acts of corruption that go unpunished and the inability of its leadership to connect meaningfully with the public.

The norms of trust-based institutions and bureaucratic efficiency are not fully embedded in the South African state. We have leaped from one system under apartheid which promoted mediocrity and corruption to another which does just the same. Thus we have what Chabal and Daloz characterise as a hybrid system, which contains elements of both informality, as found in other African states, and a façade of modern institutional features associated with modern Western states to give an impression of a commitment to some legal-bureaucratic framework.[21] Africa's elites like to be called democratic, even when democratic norms are shallow and authoritarianism or an oligarchy are deeply entrenched.

This should be unsurprising in South Africa today, given that Jacob Zuma's socio-cultural orientation is that of a traditionalist who easily mixes formal requirements of a head of state with the informality of giving his kith and kin access to the state, as if the state were an extension of his household. His philosophy of the state – if his tendencies can be called a philosophy – is a very rudimentary form of governance, an archaic conception of the state as an extension of the local setting, defined narrowly as his village – Nkandla. He runs the state by relying on a close-knit band of friends who support him financially, in the true style of patrimonial traditional authority. The totality of his purpose can be summed up as a struggle to secure personal survival.

This turns the state into what Chabal and Daloz call a 'façade masking the realities of deeply personalised political relations'.[22] If South Africa is to avoid a situation where the Big Man reigns supreme, and where the citizens are disempowered, the public would need to be vigilant and insist on strengthening the institutions that guarantee transparency and promote greater accountability.

What we have pointed out in this chapter casts the ANC as a party languishing in the throes of political death. The fall of the ANC is no longer something fanciful, but a reality waiting to happen. The depth of factionalism and the extent of corruption in the party and its government, have reached a dangerous, cancerous stage. There does not appear to be any possibility of resuscitating the ANC. The party is on its deathbed. It is understandable for observers to ask: what next?

Chapter 5

FALLING WITH PARTNERS

S peaking in London on an occasion to commemorate the 60th anniversary of the SACP on 30 July 1981, the then president of the ANC,
Oliver Tambo, had the following to say:

> *Ours is not merely a paper alliance, created at conference tables and
> formalised through the signing of documents and representing only
> an agreement of leaders. Our alliance is a living organism that has
> grown out of struggle.*

These words were uttered four years before Cosatu was formed, to add
the third component of what would be known in the South African
political lexicon as the 'tripartite alliance'.

Tambo's conceptualisation of the ANC's alliance with the SACP (and
later with Cosatu) as a 'living organism' was indeed apposite. The parts
of a living organism develop organically and they cannot be separated
from the organism without leaving it in an incomplete state. Separated
from the organism, the parts by themselves cannot live. If you cut off
the head of a living organism, all the limbs and the body of the organism must surely die. This means that when the ANC dies, as the head
of the tripartite alliance, the alliance partners must die too. Historically,
the ANC has been accepted as the leader (head) of the alliance; the

SACP and Cosatu, therefore, are the limbs of Oliver Tambo's 'living organism'.

As he was in a celebratory mood, Tambo would not, in 1981, have been thinking of the 'living organism' in terms of death. He wanted the alliance he was commemorating to live forever. Alas, his was a mere wish. The unalterable reality is that all living organisms are mortal beings that don't live forever, except in the imagination of a wishful thinker. As we have argued in the previous chapter, the ANC is falling. And, as it will become evident in this chapter, the party is not falling alone, but with the SACP and Cosatu alongside it. The whole living organism, from its head down to its limbs, is falling. The condition of each limb, however, deserves focused diagnosis.

SACP: Sucking the blood of an ANC carcass

The SACP, formerly called the Communist Party of South Africa (CPSA), was formed on 29 July 1921. From the outset, the SACP was an attachment of the Communist Party of the Soviet Union (CPSU), a puppet whose strings were pulled and whose actions were directed from Moscow. The CPSA was included in the Communist International (Comintern) conferences under the auspices of Moscow. The sixth Comintern in 1928 instructed the South African communists, along with other communist parties all over the world, 'to "bolshevise" their ranks, to fight against "Trotskyists" and right-wing opportunists'.[1] Its mission was to tighten its grip on the SACP and to convert South Africa into a socialist republic, à la the defunct Soviet Socialist Republic (SSR). Since its formation, the SACP has mutated from a white to a black to a multiracial party, depending on the whims of the CPSU leadership.

Historically, the SACP has been a small elitist organisation, led by people drunk on Marxist ideas. This elitist character was part of the design of the CPSU, which dictated: 'The Party should remain a small and select body of trained revolutionaries working through a larger mass body.'[2] As the 'larger mass body' fighting for the politico-economic liberation of the oppressed black majority, the ANC became a natural instrument to be used by the tiny SACP towards achieving its socialist ends. The SACP would use its relationships with Moscow as leverage for influence within the ANC, especially since the latter was heavily dependent on Moscow's material support for waging its struggle. In order for the ANC not to resist its influence, the SACP married its socialist objectives and the ANC's nationalist agenda. In its constitution, this is how the SACP expressed it:

> *The SACP strives to be the leading political force of the South African working class whose interests it promotes in the struggle to advance, deepen and defend the National Democratic Revolution [NDR] and to achieve socialism.*[3]

Having been instructed by Moscow to work through a 'larger mass body', and having thus engineered the SACP constitution to suit the NDR mission of the ANC, the elitist leaders of the SACP wormed their way into the upper echelons of the ANC. This was especially the case after the ANC's 1969 Morogoro conference took a decision that races other than black Africans could also be members of the ANC, a position that was heavily canvassed by members of the SACP. It is no coincidence that, historically, all prominent leaders of the SACP were also prominent leaders of the ANC. This made it easy for the SACP to influence the ideological character of the ANC. Even as there has always been a groundswell of capitalist-oriented, nationalist leaders in the ANC, the party has defined itself as a 'disciplined force of the Left'. This shows ideological preponderance by the SACP in the ANC.

Even the two-stage theory, National Democratic Revolution and socialist revolution, that became popular in the ANC and SACP was an invention in 1905 of Vladimir Lenin's. According to this formula, the struggle for socialism would be preceded by a national democratic struggle to address the 'national question' or the liberation of those oppressed under the yoke of colonialism (in the case of Russia, this was tsarist autocracy). Lenin conceived of such a government as a 'provisional revolutionary government' to ensure that the proletariat first attained political liberty. This first phase would be presided over by an assembly of people's representatives.[4]

In the context of colonised countries, a nationalist movement would install a representative parliament. Upon attaining power and instituting democratic reforms, a second revolution led by the Communist Party, supposedly a vanguard of the working class, would then be triggered. This second stage would ultimately launch an assault on the forces of 'international capital', culminating in the 'withering away' of the state and the attainment of a communist Utopia. Ironically, in contemporary South Africa the ascendance of communists to power has witnessed the withering away of socialist ideas and the emergence of strong, kleptocratic attitudes. Our communists are content with being cabinet ministers. They have neither time nor cerebral nerve for complex discussions about using the state to attain socialist ideals. On the contrary, they view the state as something to appropriate in order to dispense with patronage.

The fall of the Berlin Wall and the collapse of the Soviet Union in the late 1980s marked a fundamental disorientation of communism internationally. This led exuberant liberal intellectuals like Francis Fukuyama to declare the 'End of History'.[5] In South Africa, there was also confusion among local socialists, even goading such a towering socialist intellectual as Joe Slovo to ask, 'Has socialism failed?'[6] Although Slovo found a bogeyman in Stalinist dictatorship, the fact that socialism was in the doldrums remained unalterable.

The disintegration of the Soviet Union left the SACP ideologically like a small baby who must teach itself the ways of life because it has been abandoned in the middle of nowhere by its parents. The SACP had to find its own compass to steer its way out of the vast ideological ocean in which it found itself treading water in the 1990s. The assassination of its militant secretary-general, Chris Hani, in 1993 and the departure of Joe Slovo and his generation in 1995, left the SACP in the hands of younger, intellectually weak hotheads. The current secretary-general of the party, Blade Nzimande, is probably intellectually the weakest in the history of the SACP.

Thrown into ideological bewilderment by the collapse of the Soviet Union, and now operating in a democratic South Africa, the new generation of SACP leaders did not know what to do. Slovo's attempt to convince us that socialism had not failed was the last serious intellectual exercise since 1990. What has come from the SACP since then has been a patchwork of half-cooked slogans about socialism. Its famous slogan is: 'Socialism is the future, build it now'.[7] The thing the SACP wants to build 'now' in our country, namely, socialism, was what left millions of Russians so poor that even Russian leaders regretted ever experimenting with so bad an idea. When it finally collapsed in the Soviet Union, Boris Yeltsin almost cried tears:

> Our country has not been lucky. Indeed, it was decided to carry out this Marxist experiment on us – fate pushed us in precisely this direction. Instead of some country in Africa, they began this experiment with us. In the end we proved that there is no place for this idea. It has simply pushed us off the path the world's civilised countries have taken. This is reflected today when 40% of the people are living below the poverty level and, moreover, in constant humiliation when they receive produce upon presentation of ration cards. This is a constant humiliation, a reminder every hour that you are a slave in this country.[8]

African as he is, Blade Nzimande still does not get it. The white people of Russia think socialism should have impoverished black Africans instead of whites. But Nzimande and his fellow black communists still want South Africa, an African country, to implement what Yeltsin called a socialist ideology that reduced Russians to slaves. In short, Nzimande wants us all to be slaves, like the Russians when they implemented socialism.

The SACP has failed to craft in a democratic system a philosophical conception of what it calls 'class struggle'. As the French Marxist Louis Althusser once pontificated: 'Philosophy is, in the last instance, class struggle in the field of theory.'[9] Is there someone who knows the SACP's theory of the current South African state? Where is it?

Worst, the heirs of the SACP legacy have opportunistically accepted positions as ministers and officials in the new ANC government and have abandoned their socialist convictions. This has meant a fundamental change of class position – moving from townships to live in the capitalist conditions of the formerly white suburbs. In these changed socio-economic conditions, these so-called socialists are communists by sentiment, and capitalists by material reality.

All this is epitomised by Blade Nzimande, who, as soon as he was appointed Minister of Higher Education, was quick to use state resources to buy himself an expensive 7-Series BMW as his official vehicle, a vehicle associated with the ostentatiousness of the capitalist class. There is no modesty in this post-apartheid brand of socialists. They have learnt nothing from the pure, old-style Leftists who spent many hours studying the literature on class analysis or theory of the state and dreaming up ways of liberating the downtrodden masses.

Even before Nzimande became a minister under Jacob Zuma, his fellow communists in government had already revealed the true colours of the so-called socialists. When Thabo Mbeki was elected president, there was no shortage of Leftists in his cabinet, but these communists were not appointed on the basis of their red hats. The hats were left at Cosatu House, where the SACP is accommodated. Rather, the Leftist-leaning ministers were appointed on the strength of their credentials as

ANC leaders and capable personalities. Among them were top SACP members and leaders such as Geraldine Fraser-Moleketi, Sydney Mufamadi, Ronnie Kasrils, Essop Pahad and Jeff Radebe. Former trade union leader Alec Erwin was also a cabinet member. All of these leaders, without exception, defended Gear, the policy which sought to integrate South Africa into the global capitalist economy. Mbhazima Shilowa, another Cosatu leader and SACP member, who was known for his red socks, was appointed Gauteng premier by Mbeki, and he became a fervent defender of Gear. Who would today associate these big names with the Left or, specifically, with affiliation to the SACP? All of them left their red hats at Cosatu House.

Many socialists had their militancy tamed by the opulence which seemed to accompany their comfortable, well-recompensed government jobs. Some of them joined business. Some were put in positions which required them to implement policies that were plainly at odds with communist beliefs. Jeff Radebe, for example, was Minister of Public Enterprises, and he was constantly at loggerheads with his Leftist comrades outside government. While serving as a central committee member of the SACP, he was at the same time presiding over the privatisation of many state assets. Radebe was in charge of this portfolio at the height of the Coleman Andrews/South African Airways saga. His wife, Bridgette Radebe, is a mining entrepreneur, a proud and rich member of the black business elite.

Some of these ministers have gone on to practise what Lenin in his 1901 pamphlet 'What is to be Done?' referred to as a tendency of socialist ministers in a bourgeoisie cabinet – 'charming the whole bourgeoisie world with orations about class collaborations'.[10] Some found themselves having to defend the shooting down of the very workers of whom they claimed their party to be the vanguard. As if he had Marikana in mind, Lenin sarcastically poses the question:

Why should he [socialist minister] not remain in the cabinet even

115

after the shooting down of workers by the gendarmes has exposed, for the hundredth and thousandth time, the real nature of democratic collaborations between the classes.[11]

It is not that our socialists should worship at the base of Lenin's statue, but that they should not profess to be Leninist-Marxist when they have obviously taken an ideological leap away from such abstract ideals and have fully embraced bourgeois ideas and lifestyles themselves. Lenin would characterise our so-called socialist politicians as suffering from 'a variety of opportunism'.

As Public Service and Administration Minister, Geraldine Fraser-Moleketi, a prominent Leftist, was responsible for trimming the public service. She presided over the restructuring of the public service which, for a couple of years, saw stagnant growth in employment, to the anger of her Leftist colleagues within the SACP and public sector unions. Her husband, Jabu Moleketi, was a Leftist who increasingly became critical of the SACP and was an ardent defender of Gear. Such is the life of communists once they are in power in post-apartheid South Africa.

A number of Leftists in government were able to separate their roles as communists and ANC leaders in government with no visible signs of pain in their consciences. ANC policies were far more important and indeed realistic than the long-term utopian vision of a socialist order. In the process, many were converted, and practically became loyal disciples of Adam Smith. Rather than influencing the ANC to dump Gear, some in the Left allowed themselves to be convinced by Mbeki to eschew their criticism of the policy and to become leading spokesmen for it.

Mbeki adopted a strategy of establishing informal 'under-the-tree' discussions with left-wing leaders who had been too critical of Gear, and, through these discussions, he sought to change their thinking. Participants included some of Cosatu's most notable personalities: Gwede Mantashe and Kgalema Motlanthe, for example, from the

National Union of Mineworkers (NUM), Enoch Godongwana from the National Union of Metalworkers of South Africa, and Vusi Nhlapo of the National Education, Health and Allied Workers Union. Mbeki also sold the idea to Shilowa who until then had been an ardent critic.

Motlanthe later remembered the effect of Mbeki's informal gatherings with this group of Leftist leaders. According to him, Mbeki performed simple sums to show how it was important to lower the budget deficit in order to reduce the interest on repayment of debts in the long term. Mbeki illustrated to the group that once the budget deficit was under control, the money that was used to finance the debt would then be released for social expenditure. 'He [Mbeki] did the sums for us, he used logic to convince us, and it worked. Once I listened to him, my position changed. And I was not the only one.'[12]

It is also important to note that among leaders of the tripartite alliance, the trend has been decidedly one way: their communist/socialist ideals were conveniently discarded. On their part, Cosatu leaders were absorbed into parliament, others accepted positions in the bureaucracy and some went to business. Cyril Ramaphosa is perhaps the shiniest example of the metamorphosis from unionism to leadership in capitalism. He is even indirectly associated with the actions of the police in gunning down Marikana workers. During the Marikana commission of inquiry, it was unearthed that Ramaphosa sent emails to the Minister of Police calling for 'concomitant' action against the miners. What followed this email was a massacre. Increasingly, Ramaphosa is known more for putting up bids to purchase buffalos worth millions of rand for his game farm than for his history as a union leader.

As Kgalema Motlanthe once remarked: 'You cannot run a business in a capitalist society on a comradely basis.'[13] Cosatu and some of its affiliates even boast their own investment arms which work on the principles of capitalism. Significantly, Motlanthe later became ANC secretary-general before being elected deputy president of the ANC and of the country. He allowed his membership of the SACP to lapse. Enoch

Godongwana is an NEC member of the ANC and was Deputy Minister for Public Enterprises and later Economic Development before resigning after he and his wife were linked to a company, Canyon Springs, that embezzled R100 million of clothing workers' pension funds. The company was half owned by a family trust belonging to the Godongwanas.

On retirement from NUM, Gwede Mantashe was appointed to the Development Bank of Southern Africa (DBSA), and was co-opted into Mbeki's new policy drives, Accelerated and Shared Growth Initiative for South Africa (AsgiSA) and the Joint Initiative on Priority Skills Acquisition (Jipsa). Soon thereafter he was elected chairman of the SACP, where he seems to have rediscovered his radicalism and factional tendencies. He quit the DBSA and Jipsa posts after he was elected ANC secretary-general in Polokwane. Few now remember that Mantashe was very recently a close Mbeki-ite.

Given the behaviour of these new so-called socialists, it is not surprising that there is strong criticism from some quarters of the Left, suggesting that by associating itself with the ANC, the SACP is compromising its socialist ideals and has allowed itself to be 'corporatised' into submission by the capitalist camp of the ANC bourgeoisie. This strand of Leftist analysis does shed light on the new character of the SACP. The strand can be summarised in the words of David P. Thomas, a Canadian academic:[14]

> *As the SACP is embedded within the ruling ANC, the party's [SACP's] attempts to critique and fight neo-liberalism have remained rhetorical and ineffective. Rather than directly confronting the neo-liberal policies of the ANC, the SACP has instead co-operated with the ANC, hoping to pull it more to the left. The SACP's dedication to influencing the ANC has come at the expense of building a mass base of support that opposes neo-liberalism. This approach has ultimately resulted in an accommodation of neo-liberalism and exposes many difficult contradictions for the SACP.*[14]

The SACP has adopted an adversarial attitude towards this strand of analysis, characterising those who argue from this perspective as ultra-Leftists. In the current context of an SACP secretary-general who enjoys all the perks that ministerial office gives him, and other SACP ministers in cabinet who have said nothing against the spending of more than R200 million of taxpayers' money renovating Jacob Zuma's private compound in Nkandla, perhaps it is not surprising that anyone who criticises the leadership of the SACP faces the wrath of Blade Nzimande and his ministerial comrades.

Whatever the benefiting SACP ministers may say, what is clear is that the SACP is firmly part of the ANC's internal factional battles. In any case, Blade Nzimande is a member of the ANC's NEC. How could he not be part of the ANC's factions? Hailing from KwaZulu-Natal, Nzimande has not hidden his support for Jacob Zuma and so his loud silence on the topic of Zuma's alleged corruption shouldn't be surprising to us either. He even broached the weird idea of introducing anti-insult laws in South Africa to protect the president from critics. At the core, Nzimande is a Zulu nationalist masquerading as a socialist, who nevertheless displays very strong and conspicuous capitalist tastes. His sentimental attachment to socialism is nothing but a cover for his love of the finer things in life.

Given the ideological confusion of the SACP and the extent to which the party has become embroiled in the ANC's factional dog-fighting, the party is doomed to sink with the ANC. It does not matter how incorrigible the ANC is, the SACP will defend it, for the leadership of the party would be nothing without the ANC. In truth, the SACP is not a party preoccupied with the advancement of the interests of the working class; it is a coterie of careerists riding on the back of the ANC's access to state power. It is a parasite sucking the blood of the ANC carcass. Indeed, the ANC's poisoned blood is sure to kill the parasite, too.

Cosatu: Independence sold

When Cosatu was launched in Durban on 1 December 1985, the unions that came together to form the federation were united by their opposition to apartheid and their common aspiration to improve the working conditions of their members in a democratic, non-racial and non-sexist South Africa. Given this, it is not surprising that the new labour federation would associate itself with the biggest liberation movement, the ANC, which was working towards similar political objectives.

The 1980s was a decade of heightened political activity in South Africa. It was a time when a range of NGOs joined efforts to combat apartheid under the rubric of the UDF. On 10 October 1984, the then president of the ANC, Oliver Tambo, called upon all forces working for democracy to 'make South Africa ungovernable', further declaring on the ANC's Radio Freedom:

> We are marking two important occasions in the history of our protracted struggle at a time when the revolutionary fervour amongst all sections of the black oppressed majority has reached unprecedented heights and has plunged the ruling racist cliques into deeper and deeper levels of political and economic crisis.[15]

Tambo was right. By the 1980s apartheid had virtually reached a dead end. The international community had turned against Pretoria. Sanctions were biting and local political activists showed even greater determination to mobilise against the system.

In this political atmosphere, it was tempting for a new labour federation, which had been formed specifically to fight for workers' rights and contribute to the liberation struggle, to view the ANC as a trusted political partner of the future. What the founders of Cosatu did not take into account was the fact that the unity of protest is much stronger than the unity of governing. When various formations protest, they may differ on tactics and strategy, but the objective – which, in the case of the democratic forces of the 1980s was to overthrow apartheid – is simple and clear. Once in government, the forces of protest begin to voice different ideas as to what is to be done. Under conditions of freedom, strategic visions become hazier and tactics become fierce sources of contest. Narrow interests take precedence over common goals. To harmonise a multiplicity of interests in a free society is an almost impossible task.

This became manifest as early as 1994, when Cosatu insisted that the RDP was to be the economic policy of the new ANC government. There were some among the leaders of the ANC who thought that the RDP wish list was unworkable. Hardly three years after its adoption, the RDP was replaced, in 1996, by the Gear policy. As we have discussed in Chapter 2, Gear was criticised by Cosatu leaders as a neo-liberal policy. Ever since then, relations between the ANC and Cosatu have not been healthy, although the public has always been fed an image of unity. This image is a manufactured one, however. Beneath the façade of unity, the various parts of Tambo's 'living organism' are pulling in different directions. In a crude use of patronage, the strategy on the part of the ANC leadership has been, from time to time, to co-opt Cosatu leaders into positions of power in the ANC and in government. Being co-opted into a smart government office that gives a Cosatu activist a sizeable salary and other material benefits would indeed be very tempting. Few political angels would resist it.

The problem with the co-option strategy of the ANC is that it leaves others outside the tent. Those who are left out project themselves as the true custodians of the interests of the working class, and insinuate that the insiders have committed class suicide. Those who are in government feel that Cosatu leaders who criticise government from outside simply do not know what they are talking about, and are in cahoots with the 'liberal offensive' in the form of the Democratic Alliance. Without the leaders realising it, Cosatu has in the process been getting

torn along the lines of ANC factions. This is how Zwelinzima Vavi ultimately jumped onto the bandwagon that installed Jacob Zuma as the
president of the ANC and of the state.

Once Zuma was in the Union Buildings, most Cosatu members
were misled into believing that everything they had hoped for would
be translated into reality. Alas, they were wrong. In 2010, Vavi was thoroughly disgruntled, accusing Jacob Zuma's government of taking South
Africa in the direction of a kleptocratic state. 'We are headed for a pred-
ator state where a powerful, corrupt and demagogic elite of political
hyenas are increasingly using the state to get rich,'[16] Vavi proclaimed.

It was because of Vavi's hard stance on corruption that his fellow
comrades in Cosatu, aligned to Jacob Zuma's faction in the ANC, began
working against him. Vavi's sex scandal in 2013 came like manna from
heaven for Zuma and his lieutenants in Cosatu. Ironically, Vavi was
subjected to the same factional purging to which he and those supporting Zuma had subjected the then Cosatu president, Willie Madisha,
only a few years before. Vavi was made to taste his own bitter medicine.

The factional saga confirms one thing: the founders of Cosatu in 1985
were shortsighted in imagining the ANC as a trusted political partner
in a future democratic government. Vavi must now realise how dangerous it was for him and his comrades in Cosatu to sell the political independence of their trade union federation to a ruling party. As a trade
union, Cosatu has done well in mobilising more than 2 million members into its ranks. Now, however, it is all falling apart under the weight
of the ANC's internal factional battles.

What the founders of Cosatu did not realise was that, by entering
into an alliance with the ANC, which was set to govern, the labour
federation was *ipso facto* entering into an alliance with its employer. In
industrial relations, conflicts between employer and employee are an
objective reality. As a labour federation, Cosatu is objectively bound
to irk the ANC government. When this happens, the ANC's response
is either to summon union leaders to the party headquarters and tell

them to stop or, if this does not work, adopt the always effective strategy of divide and rule. The ANC's method of handling the irksome employee is to isolate and punish 'problematic' Cosatu leaders, and reward pliable ones.

The ANC also has vested interests in the private sector. Even as the party may pretend to be left-leaning, the subjective reality is that, as a governing party, the ANC does not want chaos in the economy. Yes, the party would like workers to be paid decent wages, but it will not tolerate protracted strikes which paint South Africa in a bad light. This is why the ANC is unhappy about the Association of Mineworkers and Construction Union (Amcu), which is not in the Cosatu fold. It cannot control Amcu.

The events leading to the Marikana massacre in 2012 best epitomise this. The Cosatu-affiliated National Union of Mineworkers (NUM) had a gentlemen's deal with mine bosses, supported by the ANC. The wage deal that Lonmin had with NUM, upset by Amcu in 2012, is the perfect example of this. (It should be noted that Amcu is now the official majority union at Lonmin, a mine previously under the dominance of NUM.) This exploitative gentlemen's deal was unacceptable to underpaid mineworkers. It must be noted that NUM leaders received salaries from mining companies. Workers could not accept this dealing and wheeling among mine bosses, the ANC government and NUM; and so they revolted. The response of the police was to massacre workers. The ANC and its sweetheart union, NUM, did not attend the event commemorating the Marikana massacre in August 2013. Must we be surprised, then, that as the ANC falls apart, NUM is also falling apart?

The seeds of Cosatu's eventual destruction were already there when the federation was formed. If, from the beginning, Cosatu had not aligned itself with the ANC, or if it had only entered into a tactical alliance, destined to come to an end with the advent of democracy, the federation would in all likelihood have been insulated from the ANC's disruptive factional battles. Had this happened, Cosatu would simply have behaved like a typical trade union: always there to put pressure on government to legislate and govern in favour of the interests of workers, and to ensure that employers treat workers fairly. This is the core business of any normal labour union. With the power to strike, the government would never ignore the demands of as powerful a labour federation as Cosatu. Alas, Cosatu founders chose to go to bed with the employer: the ANC. As a result, the federation now faces the very fate that is confronting the ANC – disintegration into irrelevance. When this finally happens, Cosatu members can blame the founders who sold the political independence of their beloved federation.

ANC leagues: Children with defective genes

The ANC Youth League (ANCYL) and Women's League (ANCWL) are the weakest in the alliance, for they cannot act autonomously against their mother body. Their constitutions are wholly subordinate to that of the ANC, even though the leagues sometimes pretend to have some political power. Without the ANC, there can be no ANC leagues. The leagues are ANC property. They can be dissolved by the ANC whenever the leadership of the mother body feels like it. Essentially, the leagues are lobby instruments inside the ANC and they are mobilisation tools for the mother body outside the party. They always dance on eggs to avoid overstepping the ANC mark.

Given its history of radicalism in the 1940s and 50s, after 1994 the ANCYL mustered the courage to make pronouncements that offended the leadership of the ANC. But the mother body leadership has always prevailed. During Mandela's presidency, Peter Mokaba, probably the most radical of all ANCYL presidents after 1994, insisted on chanting the 'Kill the Boer, Kill the Farmer' slogan when Mandela was busy preaching national unity and reconciliation. Mandela summoned Mokaba and instructed him to stop it, and, indeed, he stopped.

Malusi Gigaba's ANCYL was the sweetest in its deference to the leadership of the ANC. Plucked from obscurity, Gigaba was known for styling himself after Mbeki, even mimicking his manner of speaking. After Gigaba's presidency, Fikile Mbalula took over and tried to inject a measure of radicalism into his engagement within the ANC, but he didn't cross the line until it was clear that Thabo Mbeki was on his way out of the ANC presidency. Only then did Mbalula and his ANCYL comrades jump onto the Jacob Zuma bandwagon on the road to the chaotic ANC Polokwane conference of 2007. But on the whole, radical as he pretended to be, Mbalula was a fairly well-behaved leader of the ANCYL.

Inspired by his tribesman, Mokaba, Julius Malema went to the extreme, insulting ANC leaders at will, squaring up first to Mbeki and later to Zuma. When he was busy insulting Mbeki, Zuma condoned this by his silence, but when he did it to Zuma, Malema was expelled from the ANC. Since Malema's expulsion, the ANCYL has been virtually dead. Those in the leadership are lame ducks and stooges assembled together by Zuma when he was certain that Malema, as far as the ANC went, was history. Having seen what happened to Malema, these stooges know only too well what will happen to them if they are to mimic a modicum of Malema's radicalism. As a consequence, they are very well behaved.

The ANCYL has been the closest in resembling the mother body. While the ANC institutionalised corruption through its investment arm, Chancellor House, the ANCYL also created its own corruption cow to milk: Lembede Investment Holdings (LIH). Through LIH, the late Brett Kebble, who might have been described as the king of corruption, some leaders of the ANCYL became instantaneously rich. Kebble allegedly enriched ANCYL leaders such as Andile Nkuhlu, Songezo Mjongile and others. This could be interpreted as an attempt by Kebble to buy political influence. It got to a point when LIH was an embarrassing liability to the ANCYL, but, by the time Julius Malema and his comrades decided to wind it down, they had already devised new ways, mainly through tenders, of accessing state money. At the age of 28, having not worked in his young life, Malema was already a millionaire. Coincidentally, his material gains rose at the same time as the coffers of Limpopo province were plundered, prompting the intervention of the National Treasury.

When Malema fell out with Jacob Zuma, the taxman was unleashed upon him – the young politician, it seemed, owed SARS about R16 million. How he had made such a fortune at such a tender age as to owe so much tax still boggles the mind. Today, Malema is working very hard to convince the gullible that he is a genuine revolutionary on the side of the poor. What is clear, though, is that the ANCYL learnt a great deal about corruption from the ANC.

Since 1994 the ANC Women's League has not quite defined a unique character in the ANC for itself; it is there only to endorse ANC leaders who seem to be on the winning side. It never opposed Mandela's election to the party presidency, nor did it oppose Mbeki's election to his first and second terms as party president. The ANCWL also supported Zuma when it was clear that he was unstoppable. The case of Zuma exposed the toothlessness of the ANCWL badly. Before he was elected ANC president, Zuma was embroiled in an embarrassing rape prosecution with damaging implications for women, but the league supported Zuma nonetheless. To be frank, the ANCWL is as good as non-existent. It is really just a political tool for factional battles in the ANC.

The common feature between the ANCYL and the ANCWL is that they are both directly affected by the internal factions of the ANC. They are quick to take sides whenever there is a leadership tussle within the party. The ANCYL has often pretended to be the kingmaker, which essentially means that its preferred factional candidate ultimately takes over the leadership of the ANC, but the ANCYL is not different from the ANCWL. Both are factional instruments of those who choose to use them within the ANC. In a nutshell, the leagues of the ANC are children who have inherited the defective genes of their parent. Therefore, the leagues are bound to die like their parent – in a terrible factional accident.

Dying with its limbs

We are back to the starting point, confronted with the 'living organism' Oliver Tambo celebrated in London in 1981: the alliance. The difference now is that, as we confront it today, it is a gigantic cripple that is falling down. Tambo's 'living organism' is squirming on its deathbed, gasping for air in what are arguably its last moments. The head – the ANC – is in serious trouble. It really is a shadow of its former self. The rest lies buried in a glorified history, incapable of rescuing the battered image of the party today. If Tambo was still alive, he would, as an educated man, know that it is impossible for the head of a living organism to die without the limbs also dying. As the limbs of the ANC, Cosatu and the SACP will blow up the minute the head finally drops. What a sad ending!

Chapter 6

THE WAVE OF POST-COLONIAL AFRICAN POLITICS

Being a liberation movement in Africa, the ANC needs to be placed in the context of the African political experience in order for the organisation's performance in post-apartheid South Africa to be understood. Like other continents, Africa is politically diverse. Simplistic conclusions cannot be drawn easily about African politics. We should therefore be wary of those who counsel simplicity and try to convince us that nothing is complex in African politics. In reality, what appears simple may not be simple, for appearance is sometimes not a true reflection of an inner complexity. Intricate dynamics are at work beneath what the eye can see.

At the same time, we should not dismiss the many theories that lay claim to explaining the challenges of the continent; we should pay attention to them. It is important to examine and propound theories in order to make sense of the complex reality in which we live. Karl Popper exhorts us to remember that the value of a theory lies in its refutability, and thus, according to Popper, great lessons abound in the erroneous character of theories:

> *All theories are trials; they are tentative hypotheses, tried out to see whether they work; and all experimental corroboration is simply the*

result of tests undertaken in a critical spirit, in an attempt to find out where our theories err.[1]

Were this not the case, the field of theory would not be different from the world of dogma, where untested hypotheses parade as gospel truth. There is value in theories, refutable as they inherently are.

In the critical spirit recommended by Popper, we offer in this chapter our theory of the wave of politics to suggest that the evolution of the ANC in post-apartheid South Africa very much reflects the experiences of other post-colonial African countries. The most important thing here is not the wave theory itself; the theory is merely a facility enabling us to construct a coherent narrative.

What, then, is the essence of our wave theory of post-colonial African politics? A wave at sea appears high when it approaches the shore; it falls when it reaches the shore; and it ebbs when it loses momentum. As we will show, the political character of the post-colonial African experience closely resembles the motion of the wave: rising in the optimism that accompanies the early years of independence; falling when citizens realise that the dream of liberation was a chimera; ebbing when people lose hope. Accordingly, the politics of South Africa in the first two decades of democracy has unfolded very much in sync with the wave character of post-colonial Africa.[2]

The high wave

In 1957 Ghana led the African wave of independence from colonialism. It was a time of great optimism. There were real expectations that the colonial masters would relinquish their hold on more African countries. Indeed, the masters realised that they could not resist the winds of change, so they packed their bags and left their former colonies behind. Within a year, 1960, 17 sub-Saharan African countries gained independence and many more followed in the two decades thereafter.

Kwame Nkrumah was not a hero only in Ghana; he was regarded as the leader of the whole continent. This was not for nothing, for Nkrumah, even before the independence of his country, was preoccupied with the question of colonialism as it affected the rest of the African continent. He said:

> In 1942 when I was a student in the United States of America, I was so revolted by the ruthless colonial exploitation and political repression of the people of Africa that I knew no peace.[3]

It was this pan-Africanist outlook that led Nkrumah later to declare that the independence of Ghana meant nothing if the rest of the African continent remained under colonialism.

The decolonisation of more and more African countries in the 1960s deepened feelings of optimism and collectivism on the part of Africans. More leaders joined Nkrumah on the list of heroes associated with Africa's liberation struggle. Among others, these included Gamal Abdel Nasser of Egypt, Patrice Lumumba of Congo Zaire, Julius Nyerere of Tanzania, Jomo Kenyatta of Kenya, and Kenneth Kaunda of Zambia.

History has reserved a special place for these leaders as trailblazers in the titanic anti-colonial struggles of the peoples of Africa. They were worshipped by the people as little gods on Earth. From ordinary citizens to the media, there was an air of deference to these leaders. Anyone who dared to be critical would be reminded of the sacrifices these leaders had made in delivering freedom. So it was not that the people fought for their freedom, but the whole thing got turned on its head: the Big Men delivered liberation on a platter, and for this, citizens should be grateful.

The formation of the Organisation of African Unity (OAU) in 1963 gave practical expression to the spirit of pan-Africanism. In addition, it gave further impetus to the determination to free the entire continent. Thus the OAU was used as an instrument to assist African countries that were still languishing under the yoke of colonialism to achieve their own national liberation. This struggle was to continue until the oppressed people of South Africa were liberated from apartheid in 1994.

The OAU played an important role in supporting the political work of the liberation movement of South Africa. In a way, South Africa's freedom from apartheid concluded its liberation business. Today, only the people of Western Sahara remain colonised – strangely, by another African country, Morocco.

Essentially, the struggle against colonialism represented the yearning of Africans to be free. Its success inspired immense hope. Under the inspiration of nationalist leaders, the African masses were made to imagine a better life in their post-colonial countries. This was why they supported and participated in anti-colonial struggles. Declarations of independence were greeted with jubilation all over the continent, and the expectation of Utopia seemed like a real possibility. This marked the high point of the African wave of excitement generated by decolonisation. The future appeared blissful.

Like a wave, almost all African countries began their post-colonial political life on a high note. Given the history of colonial oppression and the gallant struggles waged by the liberation movements against racial oppression, ordinary Africans invariably expected their liberation heroes to do the opposite of what their colonisers had done in governing their countries.

When the wave is high, in the early days of independence, triumphalism characterises the national mood, and dreams seem like real prospects. Many people imagine a better time ahead, a time when there is peace and stability, an exemplary political leadership, a people-centred and corruption-free government, a collective resolve and efforts to improve the lives of poor citizens, a liberated citizenry and a winning nation. Africans from all post-colonial countries once experienced this feeling: from Ghanaians in the late 1950s to South Africans in the mid-1990s. This was when the wave was riding high.

The high wave is normally characterised by a collective sense of euphoria and a general willingness to talk about what needs to be done. This usually happens while the new government slowly settles into office and, at this stage, those who hold positions in the new government participate honestly in national discourse. At this stage, there is no imagining that the new rulers could be the next oppressors. Their skin colour serves to inoculate any critical thought. Pulling out the ticket of pan-Africanism or nationalism is sufficient for the new rulers to assure their people that all will be fine. This is the stage when the new rulers still think like political activists, riding on the wave of triumphalism and popular support. It is a time when the material gap between leaders and ordinary citizens is still a narrow one. The main difference between ordinary people and leaders is the level of political consciousness, as leaders generally come from the educated stratum of society.

The period of the high wave in African politics is essentially a period of great promise. It is a time before leaders lose their innocence and citizens cease to view reality through rose-tinted lenses. Given their heroic role and personal sacrifices made during the national liberation struggle, ordinary masses have no reason to suspect that it is possible for their leaders ever to tread upon their dreams and aspirations. This period is characterised by a great deal of wishful thinking and naivety. The promises made by leaders are viewed by many in society as things waiting to happen, even though most of the promises are informed by a sheer lack of experience on the part of the nationalist leaders and the people themselves. When the wave is high, Utopia looks like the place people will live in. Alas, it does not happen.

When the wave falls

The period of the high wave does not last long. It is soon followed by a calamitous decline. The beginning of the decline is marked by a set of complex circumstances. It can take place in a political environment characterised by violence or in a relatively peaceful atmosphere. But, eventually, the essential features of a country which has experienced the fall of the wave are very similar. The violent or peaceful ways in which the decline expresses itself are simply different routes to the same destination: disaster.

The violent fall of the wave has been the commonest in Africa's post-colonial political experience. No sooner have ordinary people finished celebrating the miracle of independence than an announcement is made on national television or radio that the post-colonial government has been toppled. This will generally be announced by some military junta. Ironically, the country that led the wave of independence in Africa, Ghana, experienced exactly this hardly ten years after independence.

On 24 February 1966 an announcement was made on Radio Ghana that the military had taken over the government of Ghana. This declaration was made while the man known as the 'Father of African Nationalism', Kwame Nkrumah, was visiting Beijing, a very interesting choice of country since he regarded himself as the African Lenin. His removal was effected in a bloodless coup d'état. From 1966 until his death in 1972, Nkrumah did not live in Ghana, the country he had worked to liberate. He was hosted in exile by his friend Sékou Touré, then president of Guinea. Nkrumah, the great pan-Africanist, loved and adored by many in Africa, ended his political life a miserable man in a foreign land.

Today, when the story of Nkrumah is told, it is as if history were ungrateful to him. In fact, a great deal of reconstructionist efforts have been made by his admirers to rescue his image and recast Nkrumah in a positive light. In the process, however, the truth becomes the victim. While the military generals who overthrew Nkrumah certainly had their own ulterior motives, Nkrumah also had a hand in his own destruction. Once he was in power in Ghana, it did not take long before this great liberator revealed his despotic streak. He was ruthless against opposition politicians and had no regard for democratic politics. He lived for power.

Given that this was the first African country to be liberated, one would have expected it to be the best example of democracy and liberty from an African perspective. Alas, Ghana, under the revered Nkrumah, took the road to dictatorship. In 1964 Nkrumah declared Ghana a single-party state, essentially installing his own party, the Convention People's Party, as the only party to rule Ghana. He then declared himself president for life. But it was not to be; he was kicked unceremoniously out of power.

The political story of Ghana is a story of betrayed hopes. The man who had inspired millions of people to expect a better life under a government led by their own African leaders was the same man who put in place a despotic regime after independence. Instead of political freedom and economic prosperity, the people of Ghana, under Nkrumah, were subjected to dictatorship and, even worse, to economic hardship. By the time Nkrumah was toppled, he had already ravaged the economy of his country by experimenting with reckless socialist ideas. He was accountable to no one, and had nothing substantive to show for his earlier ideals.

For years following Nkrumah's dethronement, the people of Ghana were pummelled by the rough winds of sham democracy and military rule. Real hope for democracy returned with the 1992 elections, following decades of political mayhem.

In the same way that Ghana led the way to independence, it was also among the first countries on the continent to betray the hopes of its people. Other African leaders learned a great deal from Nkrumah.

Rebels also learned important lessons from the generals who toppled him. Thus, Ghana's mayhem of military interventions and coups d'état were reproduced across the continent. Most of Africa began to enjoy semblances of democratic rule after 1990, even as a few political hotspots remained, such as Somalia, Rwanda, Burundi, and the Democratic Republic of the Congo.

Terrible as the Ghanaian experience was, it was not the worst in Africa. There are many similar experiences of the betrayal of hope. That of the former Congo Zaire (now the Democratic Republic of the Congo) is one of the most heartbreaking. Following the violence that led to the death of the revered nationalist leader, Patrice Lumumba, the country was ruled for 32 years by a very backward army officer, Mobutu Sese Seko. During these long years, Zaire witnessed the most horrendous forms of misrule and the economic plundering of the country. In fact, 'backward' is an understatement in relation to Mobutu, who is among the worst kleptocrats the African continent has ever known. This is how the whole world knows him: as a kleptocratic dictator who represented Africa's backwardness in leadership.

There is hardly a political evil that Zaire did not witness under Mobutu, from the slaying of political opponents to the privatisation of the whole state by a single individual. When his pockets were full of looted money, Mobutu even advised public servants to steal: 'Go ahead and steal, as long as you don't take too much.'[4] If this was not madness, then madness has no meaning.

Following independence, Africans did not only experience violence by military dictators. There are countries on the continent which have generally been peaceful and were not run by the military. Yet the wave of excitement generated by independence also ebbed for the citizens of such countries. The case of Kenya illustrates this point poignantly.

Until the ethnic violence that erupted following the presidential election of 2007, Kenya had been a relatively peaceful country. Given the political volatility of the East African sub-region, this country was an island of peace in a troubled ocean in spite of its ethnic divisions. Yet this island of peace was at the same time a political volcano waiting to erupt. Since the death of the heroic Jomo Kenyatta and until the 2002 elections, Kenya had been a peaceful dictatorship under an accomplished kleptocrat, Daniel arap Moi.

Under Moi, Kenyans went through tribulations. Underestimated when he took over from Kenyatta in 1978, Moi gradually established himself among the most sophisticated dictators in Africa. Operating in the context of relative peace, he constructed a pliable political architecture that made it easy for him to pull strings like a puppet master. Matters got to a point where this accomplished dictator could even determine the hiring and firing of professors at universities. Professor Shadrack Gutto, the well-known law professor, fled Kenya by the skin of his teeth. As an independent critic, Gutto had offended Moi to the extent that people advised Gutto to flee his country – or else he could have disappeared forever. The disappearance of government critics was a usual occurrence under Moi. In their so-called peaceful country Kenyans lived in fear.

The political tragedy of this beautiful East African country is perfectly parodied in the novel by acclaimed African writer Ngũgĩ wa Thiong'o, *Wizard of the Crow*, in which ministers are said to have gone to Europe to have their eyes, ears and tongues enlarged so that they could see better, hear more and issue louder commands on behalf of the ruler.[5] Such was the sophistication of Daniel arap Moi that old, rational men offered themselves as loyal henchmen in the service of a vain dictator who occasionally fancied himself a 'professor of politics' – although Moi's last professional job was as a school teacher.

When Kenya blew up in ethnic violence in 2007/08, few observers could make a connection between retired president Moi and the violence, but the connection was more than strong. At the centre of the violence lay a deep mistrust of the public institutions to which all Kenyans ought to have turned in times of politico-legal disputes. However,

Moi's job of delegitimising courts of law and other legal instruments had been so perfect that, when the 2007/08 violence erupted, not even a madman could have detected a whiff of legitimacy in the country's public institutions. When public institutions that are supposed to hold society together have been subordinated to sectional political interests, chaos is sure to follow. This is precisely what happened in 2007/08 in Kenya. It was the upshot of many years of misrule by a post-colonial regime that had promised freedom and prosperity to its people.

The case of Zimbabwe is too fresh in the collective memory of Africans. In 1980, Robert Mugabe styled himself as a champion of the rule of law, declaring: 'Only a government that subjects itself to the rule of law has any moral right to demand of its citizens obedience to the rule of law.'[6] Fast forward to the 2000s. Mugabe became known by the rest of the world as one of the most brazen destroyers of the rule of law. Zimbabweans who had viewed Mugabe in the early days of independence as someone who would bring prosperity and stability were painfully disappointed by a man who later brought hunger and strife to a country once known as the food basket of southern Africa. In January 2013, Zimbabwe's colourful Finance Minister Tendai Biti shocked the world when he announced publicly that, after paying public servants, Zimbabwe's public account was left with a paltry $217. It would be amusing were it not so tragic.

Mugabe continues to be celebrated by some as a post-colonial hero, despite the fact that he has condemned millions of black Zimbabweans to exile. Public services have collapsed in that country, infrastructure is creaking, and over 70% of its population has no formal employment. The rhetoric about anti-imperialism and land redistribution has pulled the wool over the eyes of many Zimbabweans, who hold up Mugabe and his half-cooked policies as a model for economic prosperity. In South Africa, he is a hero for many who are frustrated at the slow pace of economic transformation in their own country, yet they would not trade their place in South Africa to live under Mugabe's ruthless rule.

When emotions blunt the capacity to reason, dictators thrive. And this is the story for much of the continent.

Even countries which have not witnessed such dramatic periods of misrule have very little to show as the socio-economic dividends of their much-celebrated independence. The early leaders of Zambia and Tanzania – Kenneth Kaunda and Julius Nyerere respectively – were in the main well-meaning and honest human beings. While they did their best to improve the lives of their people, they also had their moments of economic folly. Nyerere, for example, toyed with *Ujamaa* (African socialism), which left Tanzania as under-developed as it was before he implemented his lofty ideology. This was a step in the wrong direction.

In 1969, Kaunda nationalised copper mines in Zambia. This was yet another wrong step. He abandoned this fruitless socialist policy in the 1980s, when his people were evidently getting poorer. Political independence has certainly boosted the national ego of the people of Zambia and Tanzania, but these people continue to wait for the elusive economic benefits of their independence.

The recent political upheavals in North Africa – the so-called Arab Spring – were a rude reminder that the people will not wait for a miracle to deliver them from sham democracy and poverty. It gets to the point where ordinary people realise that they have it within their power to change their own circumstances, to confront mighty armies with mere stones and a courageous spirit, to bring down the fortresses of dictators who fancy themselves invincible. Everyone who has watched events in Tunisia, Egypt and Libya in the recent past knows that this is true.

In most countries where political independence has not produced practical economic outcomes for the masses of the downtrodden, well-fed politicians and well-connected intellectuals are very vocal about the importance of independence. In the comfort of their plush offices, they manufacture self-serving illusions of progress in the post-colonial era, but in reality they are the only ones who are experiencing the so-called progress. For the millions of the poor, progress is only experienced in the form of slogans crafted by cunning, urban-based intellectuals and rich politicians. The intellectuals who busy themselves in their factories, manufacturing slogans, forget Amílcar Cabral's profound counsel:

> Always bear in mind that the people are not fighting for ideas, for the things in anyone's head. They are fighting to win material benefits, to live better and in peace, to see their lives go forward, to guarantee the future of their children.[7]

This is how the wave of African politics drops. It is a stage when the practical experiences of the hopeful people of a post-colonial country tell a story different from that narrated by those who hold positions of power. It is a time when the animals on Orwell's farm begin to realise that while 'all animals are equal, some animals are more equal than others'.[8] At this stage, the people begin to realise that while politicians exhort them to be patient, politicians themselves are busy amassing personal wealth, and looting public resources as if tomorrow will never come.

After a while, when the wave begins to fall, the poor begin to doubt that the better life promised by those in power will ever come. At this point in the life of a post-colony, serious cracks begin to reveal themselves among Africans. Race loses its potency as a source of political unity, and the seeds of scepticism begin to germinate in the soil of the governed against the new governors. Class disparities take the place of racial divisions. But the post-colonial African leadership never stops beating the drum of anti-colonialism and anti-imperialism. The more ordinary people express discontent about the misdeeds of their African leaders, the louder the leaders scream against imperialism and colonialism. The leaders and beneficiaries of their patronage do this in order to keep those twin bogeymen alive in the minds of the poor who are growing impatient and more suspicious.

The ebbing wave

When the wave flows, its boundaries are not always clear. And the stages in the evolution of Africa's post-colonial political experience are not always clear either. While some may still be twirling in the intoxication that accompanies the euphoria of liberation, native politicians may already be hard at work thieving from the state. Only after a while does a trend emerge, enabling observers to discern certain practices that define the character of the new era. Often the actors on the stage do not realise what the spectators in the theatre are seeing, for the intensity of the action may not afford the actor the vantage point enjoyed by those who watch from a distance.

The transition from one stage to the next in African politics is something similar. The beginning of the euphoria of independence is usually very clear because Independence Day is declared publicly. But the beginning of the fall is not neatly demarcated from the end of the independence euphoria.

The same holds true in respect of the ebb. In fact, the line between the fall of the wave and the beginning of the ebb is the most difficult to detect. What renders it more difficult is the fact that often those in power deploy resources deliberately to obfuscate.

The powerful in society contrive an assortment of schemes to make people believe that all is well. The most common is the use of state-owned media to communicate positive messages about those in government. The appointment of the head of the public broadcaster becomes a high-stakes affair. Whoever gets the job must be someone vetted thoroughly by party apparatchiks to ensure that nothing comes from the state broadcaster that might embarrass the governing party. Journalists with an independent streak are either silenced or pushed out. The journalists who survive are the pliable ones, those who are concerned chiefly with their material comfort or have aligned opportunistically to governing party politics. In the end, the whole public broadcaster is synchronised with the party. Ministers of information, who are usually members of the politburos of governing parties, become *de facto* heads of the state broadcaster, always ready to protect the image of the party.

Concomitant to distortions within the state broadcaster are stratagems to emasculate independent media. The intention is to ensure that all channels of mass communication are controlled wholly by the state and thereby by the political party in power. Independent media in most post-colonial African countries are established by people who can see through the intentions of politicians regarding the state broadcaster. Soon independent-minded thinkers and commentators find an alternative voice through independent media.

Understandably, this is not tolerated by those in power. It does not take long before politicians devise dirty tricks to silence alternative voices. This is mainly done through legislative means or other forms of executive decree. Thus the public is misled through the media to believe that the country is in good hands and good shape. The objective of those in power is to ensure that the people do not realise that the country is sliding down the slippery slope of misrule.

Power, therefore, is maintained through fantasy. In a way, the people are hypnotised and made to feel as though they exist in a wonderful world of paradise, a world that is detached from the concrete, grinding actuality of their daily lives. The heroic trumpet of the liberation struggle is blown so hard as to keep echoing in the heads of the poor masses, as if the people will turn the gallantry of liberation into food to feed their children. The sad reality, though, is that the former liberation fighters, who now hold positions of power, do not live in the fantasy world; they live in a new reality of material opulence and political power. They have inherited plush offices, luxury vehicles and sumptuous houses from the colonialists, and politicians seek to maintain this lifestyle for themselves by pumping the heads of the poor full of numbing political slogans and lofty economic promises.

It is therefore not very easy to detect the lines that mark the end and beginning of the various stages in the wave of post-colonial African politics. While observers may think that they are still witnessing a decline, the ebb may very well be in full swing. Also, the fall and the ebb of the wave are inextricably connected. If there is no fall, there will be no ebb. And if there is no ebb, there would certainly have been no fall. The two are linked dialectically.

The illusiveness of the ebb is further compounded by the fact that societies never stop evolving. While a country may seem abysmal today, its current state may not of necessity be its permanent state. What we see today may tell us very little about what societies will be like 100 or even 20 years from now.

The Arab Spring provides a perfect example. Before it took place, no single political theorist foresaw it. It would have sounded like madness if anyone had suggested that, very soon, a popular uprising would be ignited by an aggrieved hawker setting himself alight, which is what happened in Tunisia. Similarly, a prophet would have been dismissed as an hallucinator in the 1970s if he suggested that, in 2014, the United States of America would be led by a black president. Here we are, living in the unthinkable future of the dead.

The difficulty about the ebb in politics is that it tells us little about the future. Does the fact that Somalia today is a failed state mean that chaos will prevail in that country until the end of time? Does the fact that Jacob Zuma is president of South Africa today mean that South Africa will be led by alleged criminals until Jesus Christ comes back? Is Syria doomed to blow up in an eternal inferno of civil war? What of Israel and Palestine? Are the mothers giving birth there certain that their children will never know peace in their whole lives? No one can answer these questions, for no one knows the future.

But the fact that we do not know the future does not mean that we do not know what happened yesterday. Nor does it mean that the mystery about the future necessarily renders us incapable of making sense of where we are today. Humans are capable of deciphering their prevailing conditions, even as they are incapable of seeing into the future. We therefore can explain the good, the bad and the worst of our times – or the follies and ingenuities of yesteryear's societies.

On the basis of what we have observed in Africa, therefore, what constitutes the ebb?

Let us recall the essence of what we described as the rise and fall of the wave of post-colonial African politics. We said that the high wave in the early days of independence is characterised by optimism and high expectations – a period when people imagine better times ahead. We further suggested that the fall of the wave is when ordinary people who had been inspired by the promise of a better future begin to lose patience and become suspicious of what politicians promise them. The ebb, therefore, is when the people no longer have hope in the political system due to the bad behaviour of politicians, civil servants or the private sector.

Sometimes there is wisdom in clichés: 'Poor people may be poor, but not stupid'. The overwhelming majority of people in post-colonial African countries are poor, but not stupid. They believe the promises made by their leaders only to a point. It gets to the stage where the people know that the mantra of 'job creation' mouthed by politicians is nothing more than hollow words. At this stage, the people simply rely on themselves, devising all sorts of means to survive. The daring among them leave their places of origin for urban environs in search of better prospects. This is what has contributed to the mushrooming of slums in most African cities. Rural dwellers cease to believe the slogans about rural development manufactured by politicians who are themselves enjoying a good life in the city. Without being instructed by politicians, ruralitarians also move to cities in search of a better life. This happens when they have lost hope in the theories and manifestos presented by politicians.

When the wave ebbs, the educated among the African people are the first to skip their countries, taking their families abroad to escape strife in the countries of their birth. When this happens, politicians back home make a lot of noise against the so-called brain drain, and the richer countries that encourage it. These politicians are hypocrites. On the one hand, they criticise richer countries for draining skills from poorer countries but, on the other hand, these same politicians are the ones who are plundering the state and corrupting the economic system of their own country to the extent that there are few economic opportunities to keep honest professionals at home.

It is disingenuous to suggest that African professionals do not love their countries; they go to work in foreign lands because their own countries offer them no opportunities. African professionals are rational human beings; they take rational decisions. If you want to keep scientists, build them a laboratory.

Unskilled citizens of post-colonial African countries also emigrate in search of economic opportunities. Richer countries on the continent and beyond have parts of their cities virtually taken over by African immigrants. Often these immigrants live in run-down parts of foreign cities. The conditions endured by the immigrants when they make their way out of their own countries suggest an escape from an extremely bad situation back home. Indeed, reports of overcrowded boats full of desperate Africans braving rough seas en route to Europe abound. This happens when the great promise of a prosperous post-colonial experience has gone belly-up.

In a post-colonial African country, where the ebb is at play, the entire state system is subordinated to the interests of those in power. State institutions have been converted to components of a mega-patronage network, overseen at the top by the head of state himself. Ministers and other officials below the head of state know only too well that they are there to look after themselves and their friends in the private sector. Corruption becomes the order of the day. It gets to the point where citizens are no longer moved by corruption scandals in the media because scandals are a daily occurrence. In such a situation, citizens know that politicians who are corrupt face no consequences. In Kenya under Daniel arap Moi, this was brazen:

> By the early 1990s, Western executives flying in with plans to invest in Kenya quickly realised that their companies would never thrive in the country's supposedly free-market environment unless a slice of equity was discreetly handed over to a firm owned by a Moi relative, trusted henchman or favoured minister.[9]

If the president himself is implicated in corruption, who will protect poor and powerless citizens? Citizens in most post-colonial African states have no faith in their heads of state, for they know that the 'Big Man' at the top is also eating. In fact, the head of state is treated like a drug lord, feared by the citizens. In such countries, presidents are close to the people only in theory; in practice, they are not. They are protected by a heavy army of presidential guards and they drive in big convoys. Whenever they make contact with ordinary people, the whole thing is choreographed and is a high-security affair – sniffer dogs will be sent to 'clean' the place where the president is scheduled to meet the people. This sort of stuff is very intimidating to ordinary folk. But such is life in a post-colonial African country experiencing an ebbing political wave.

There are those who believe in some kind of exceptionalism that supposedly differentiates South Africa from the rest of the African continent, but observers who have watched the wave of post-colonial African politics can see that what they are witnessing in South Africa today is very similar to what they saw in Kenya in the 1970s, or Ghana in the 1960s, or Zimbabwe in the 1980s. To such observers, the so-called South African exceptionalism is exposed for what it is – a lie used by those in power to deceive poor people. Viewed through the prism of the wave theory of post-colonial African politics, post-apartheid South Africa under the ANC suddenly makes sense, does it not?

Chapter 7

IS THIS THE SOCIETY THE ANC HAD IN MIND?

All political parties, whether or not they are aware of it, are social engineers. Whether or not in power, political parties have an imagined ideal society, one they aspire to create. It would be a party of mindless people that has no idea of what kind of social relations it would prefer in ordering or reordering the society in which the party operates. The imagined society (social model) of a political party is the product of its chosen political ideology. In other words, the social models preferred by parties are aligned with their political ideologies. When a party imagines a particular social model, it will adopt an ideology it believes fits in with this model.

If communists had their way, they would turn people of all societies into beings who think of their community first before they think of themselves – individuals who view themselves as cogs in a big social wheel, bound by the common ownership of land and means of production. When a communist surveys society from above, individuals dissolve into distinct social forces which determine the twists and turns of the whole social organism. Thus a social organism drifting in the direction of capitalism, according to communists, has to be re-engineered by empowering the proletariat with the consciousness of their collective exploitation in order for the working class to wage a class struggle against capitalist exploitation; so that, in the end, the social stream can flow in the direction of socialism and, ultimately, communism. Such are the social dreams of communists.

While there are different strands of liberals and indeed a variety of imagined liberal permutations of the state, the general thrust of a liberal conception of society is that of a small government, with an absolute minimum of restrictions placed upon individuals, in a society where human freedom is not burdened by the yoke of collectivism. As they look at society, liberals imagine something akin to a galaxy of loose human particles unconnected to one another apart from the fact that they occupy the same geographical space. Dis-embedded individuality is seen as more supreme than a situation where each human being is defined primarily by a social system. This is the kind of social order liberals would like to see constructed and preserved.

Indeed, very many conceptions of society exist in the space between communism and liberalism. They, too, represent the imagination of the political parties that believe in them. What remains true is that each social model is the invention of political actors. When we say that communists see social forces when they look at society, or that liberals see a loose collection of individuals, we are simply stating that what political parties see is a reflection of their own subjective social constructs and political ideals. Their social models are not the products of nature; they are schemes manufactured in the minds of people.

As social engineers, political parties are free to make their own assessment of society – that is, to see it as they choose. Indeed, politicians say many things about us South Africans, things that, as individuals, farmers, shopkeepers or fishermen, we do not see as an accurate representation of our daily experiences. But politicians continue to express their views about our reality, for such is politics: the representation of social reality with the view to maintaining or changing it. Sometimes the representations are close to what we think is real; at other times they are quite distant.

Analysis is easy; change is difficult. When political parties analyse us, we do not participate in their analysis. We simply go on with our lives while politicians try to make sense of our behaviour, and to imagine what they need to do to make us behave in line with their ideals. Change is difficult because, unlike machines in a factory, human beings are not docile participants in a social factory controlled masterfully by politicians. Human beings can and do disrupt the designs of political parties by acting in a manner that contradicts what politicians have in mind. This is the inherent imperfection of the craft of social engineering.

When we assess the state of South African society in relation to what the ANC pronounced as its social ideals, we must therefore avoid treating our society as clay in the hands of the party, ready to be moulded around the fantastic imagination of the ANC. Ours is a society of human beings who, before and after 1994, have been going about their lives on the basis of what they decide to do as individuals or groups of individuals.

It is true that oppressive governments can and do constrain the conduct of citizens in a manner that produces a social system designed by oppressors. For example, inter-racial marriages were once declared unlawful under apartheid. Under the circumstances, love did not have the freedom of choice; it had to be conscious of the skin colour of its subject and, if it defied the legal restrictions of the time, it would be punished severely. Thus the resultant society was one in which marriages between whites and blacks were rare, not because whites and blacks had no feelings for each other, but because apartheid's social engineers had suppressed people's feelings.

Similarly, under apartheid, a visitor to South Africa may have been misled to believe that blacks did not want to live in the suburbs, but observers who knew what was happening would have been aware that what they observed was a subjective social reality, constructed and maintained by apartheid's social engineers. In other words, a society without inter-racial marriages was what was in the heads of apartheid's social engineers, and this was translated into practice through legislation, thus producing a subjective practical reality.

The example of apartheid does not, however, tell the entire story of social engineering. Even under conditions of freedom, political parties, through their policies, can and do transform societies. For example, the South African government has since 1994 given millions of poor South Africans access to electricity. While it can be taken for granted, electricity is a socially transformative agent in a profound manner.

Before they had electricity, millions of South Africans living in rural areas had no access to television in their homes. This meant that they had limited access to what was happening all over the world. What they knew was transmitted, in a sifted manner, via radio. In such a social environment, it was not easy for bonds of traditions to be broken. For example, some black rural communities would declare it taboo for girls to wear pants, and, given that girls had no access to television, they would conclude that what they saw in their small rural communities was the norm across the country. As soon as television was introduced through electricity, girls in rural communities came to realise that their counterparts elsewhere did wear pants, and that it was actually 'cool' to wear pants. Thus the age-old rural traditions that women wear long dresses and skirts, and that pants were the exclusive preserve of men, were blown away by a simple thing such as television, powered by electricity.

The provision of electricity to rural communities also had other positive and negative consequences. For the first time, ruralitarians could buy refrigerators. This meant that they could now keep food in their refrigerators, which was an improvement from traditional methods of preserving food, some of which may not have been hygienic. Undoubtedly, this was a positive contribution made by electricity to the quality of life in rural areas. These are some of the positive impacts of the ANC's energy policies.

Electricity's negative consequence, though, was the destabilisation of small-scale rural entrepreneurship. Now that ruralitarians had refrigerators, most of them no longer bought meat, for example, from a local tuckshop, since they could buy in bulk for storage in their refrigerators. This meant that villagers could now buy food from big food chains in their nearest towns and keep it in their refrigerators. The owner of a small tuckshop in the village, who used to sell food to villagers, now had to compete with the big food chains in the nearest town. For this small businessman, the end was obvious: bankruptcy. This the ANC could never have planned to do. The party's mass electrification programme was certainly well-meaning, but it did have unintended social consequences.

The point we are making is that the decisions of democratic regimes do shape or reshape societies. As social engineers, political parties in democracies do announce their plans to change society in particular ways, but the change may not always be in line with the aims of those who plan to re-engineer society. Under conditions of freedom, citizens do not just comply with the designs of political parties; as free agents, they often do their own things. That the social engineering policies of political parties, particularly governing parties, do yield outcomes not intended by the parties begs the question: does South African society today reflect what the ANC had in mind when it made a commitment to transform society 20 years ago?

In other words, has the ANC succeeded in moulding social relations around its own objectives? This question cannot be answered without first dealing with another question: what are the social objectives that the ANC sought to achieve in a new democratic society? Clearly, such objectives must have been informed, in the first place, by what the ANC thought was wrong with South African society as it was constituted during apartheid.

The social engineering of racism

As we have pointed out in Chapter 1, apartheid was not the first, out-of-the-blue racist experiment in South Africa, or indeed in the world. It was part of very old racist traditions in the Occident, traditions that have for centuries made white mercantilists view Africans as sub-humans who are worthy of enslavement. Evidence of the age-old attitude that blacks were instruments for the advancement of white interests is well documented. In fact, there was a period when this truth was not dressed in euphemisms; it was told as bare as it is. Consider, for example, the explicit language used in 1872 by the respected British historian and explorer Winwood Reade:

> The Portuguese discovered the slave-land itself [Africa], and imported ten thousand negroes a year before the discovery of the New World. The Spaniards, who had often negro slaves in their possession, set some of them to dig in the mines at Santo Domingo: it was found that a negro's work was as much as that of four Indians, and arrangements were made for importing them from Africa.[1]

When Cecil John Rhodes and his friends germinated the seeds of what is today referred to as the South African mining industry, from the chaotic diamond diggings of Kimberley in the 1870s, their attitude was the same as that of the Spaniards in the seventeenth century: use Africans to dig out mineral resources for the benefit of Europeans. Indeed, racism in South Africa was tried and tested by successions of white settlers – from the Dutch to the British. Apartheid merely consummated a racist system whose foundations had been laid and concretised for more than 290 years.

Apartheid's social engineers had a clear purpose in mind: implement a racial scheme that would place whites at the top of South Africa's social order. This was a white supremacist agenda, resting on two fundamental pillars: firstly, the political exclusion of the African majority; and, secondly, the economic disempowerment of Africans, coloureds and people of Asian descent. To achieve this, various legislative instruments were used, such as the Population Registration Act of 1950 and the Group Areas Act of 1950. These were meant to deny blacks the privileges enjoyed by whites, such as freedom of movement and the right to choose places of abode. Education was used as an instrument of indoctrination and to buttress the racist system of apartheid. A particularly inferior education system was designed for the African majority. The Bantu Education Act of 1953 and the Extension of University Education Act of 1959, for example, were both measures meant to reproduce inferiority. Africans processed through these schemes were expected to minister to the needs of the white man.

The upshot of all this was a racially divided society, a society in which the colour of a person's skin determined his opportunities or plight. By virtue of being white a person would be entitled to clean public amenities such as toilets, parks, and so on. By virtue of being black a person would be arrested for walking in the streets of a whites-only suburb without a permit.

This was a system that institutionally drove the African majority into conditions of poverty and under-development. Africans were systematically and forcefully restricted to the lowest rung of the economic ladder. Apartheid social engineers also sought to create a society that placed women in lower positions in social, political and economic life. In the main, the designs of apartheid engineers did produce their intended racist results.

What happened to the ANC's social objectives?

The ANC came to power with a social engineering plan that sought to alter what apartheid had put in place. In other words, the ANC undertook to create a normal society where all citizens, regardless of race or sexual orientation, enjoy equal opportunities and are entitled to the same rights. This overarching social objective was expressed clearly in the Freedom Charter: 'Our country will never be prosperous or free until all our people live in brotherhood, enjoying equal rights and opportunities'.

Twenty years into democracy, do South Africans live in harmony and enjoy equal opportunities? Are they reconciled? This is not an easy question to respond to, for neither a 'yes' nor 'no' would be sufficient to represent the complexity of the society that has emerged out of the social engineering efforts of the ANC since 1994. A bigger complication arises from the problem of representation. As analysts, we are not different from the playwright, who, as Herbert Marcuse observes, is confronted

> with the question of whether it is still possible to 'represent the con-
> temporary world in the theatre' – that is, represent it in such a man-
> ner that the spectator recognises the truth which the play is to convey.[2]

When we point out the positives of the current society, the ANC would most likely welcome such a depiction as a true representation of society, and the party would embrace the positives as part of its grand social scheme to transform society. However, a reflection that brings out the negatives would elicit protest by the ANC or, if the party does not protest, it would simply disown the negatives as aberrations that have nothing to do with its social engineering designs. But we cannot shy away from the task of analysing for fear of the ANC's – or anybody else's – reaction. Complex as the task of representation is, we, like the playwright, still have the duty to represent things as we see them.

An analysis of post-apartheid South African society can be conducted on two levels: firstly, on the formal, 'legal' level; and, secondly, on the informal, 'meta-state' level. The formal level is less difficult to deal with as it is the realm defined by laws and legal regulations. For example, the following question applies to the formal level: is racism illegal in South Africa today? Answering 'yes' to such a question would be a correct representation of South African law, which matter-of-factly outlaws racism.

At the same time, such an answer would not be responding to the question: does racism exist in South Africa today? This is an equally important question, extending beyond what formal state institutions may have promulgated. It is for this reason that we call the informal level of analysis a 'meta-state' realm – a realm beyond what the state can do.

At the formal level, the ANC has made it lawful for South Africans of all races to live in the same social spaces harmoniously and to enjoy equal opportunities. Unlike what used to pertain under apartheid, it is illegal for any person to discriminate against another on the basis of race. In other words, an owner of a private shop has no right to declare his a 'whites-only' or 'Indians-only' shop. Such an act would be illegal according to the new South African law. Is racism legal in South Africa today? The answer is a simple 'no'.

Yet we know that conditions that sustain racism do still exist. Equal opportunity is a myth. Those who had the benefits of exclusive privileges in the past have continued to enjoy them even in the absence of legal infrastructure according such privileges legal status. The metaphor of life as a race is instructive in this regard. Whites have in the past been deliberately placed a thousand miles ahead of the race through social engineering. The starting point of successive generations post-apartheid is far more advantageous. They have an enduring security for success. Their station is therefore vastly different from that of the majority of blacks, even with the benefit of equity policies and ill-conceived BEE programmes.

The social infrastructure of racism, 20 years into democracy, still exists. Consider, for example, a pub owned by an Afrikaner farmer somewhere in the countryside, established in the middle of a farm for the purpose of serving as a hangout for local Afrikaner farmers. Would it not be naive to think that, given that racial discrimination has been outlawed, black farm workers in the area would now view the former-ly 'whites-only' pub as their hangout spot? Although by law this pub would be considered accessible to blacks, the racial infrastructure of the pub (that is, its history, culture and the prices of the beverages it serves) may serve as a deterrent to black farm workers who have for years regarded the pub as an exclusive space for their Afrikaner bosses. To expect a poor black farm worker suddenly to regard the pub as his own would be naivety of the highest order.

It is important to note that the infrastructure of racism does not only exist in previously whites-only areas. Formerly blacks-only residential areas themselves constitute barriers for racial integration. The idea of well-off white South Africans relocating to black townships is not dif-ferent from hallucination; it is almost impossible to conceive of. As far as whites are concerned, 1994 or no democracy, townships remain the exclusive preserve of poor blacks. In any case, such places are economi-cally poor, with many blacks dreaming of running away from them and securing better settlement in predominantly white suburbs.

However integrationist the ANC may have been, its social engineer-ing could do nothing to make whites move to historically black areas in the spirit of nation building. In this regard, the ANC's dream of an 'inclusive approach, free of arrogance or complexes of superiority or inferiority'[3] is nothing more than a pipe-dream.

Overcoming arrogance or complexes of superiority or inferiority is not a matter of legal declaration. Arrogance and complexes arise from material conditions, rich or poor conditions that make a person feel either worthless or king of the castle. However hard you may try, mak-ing a poor black person think that he is not inferior to a rich white person would be a fruitless exercise. Equally idealistic would be the psychological task of making a rich white man, who had for many years looked down upon poor black people, change his mind. Anyone who makes this their devotion is naive. Ngũgĩ wa Thiong'o's dream of decolonising the minds of Africans is an unrealistic one.

To point to the difficulties involved in the meta-state realm is not to suggest that nothing significant has been achieved through the promulgation of laws meant to transform South African society. The raft of laws introduced by the ANC-led government after 1994 has produced tangible results. In other words, the ANC's mega-social engineering project has redefined the country's social landscape.

The legal removal of racial barriers has facilitated a move by black people who have the financial means to do so to migrate from places historically designated 'blacks-only' to historically white suburbs. Few as they are, such black people have experienced, in a real sense, the meaning of the ANC's promise of equal opportunities. Unlike before, the black elite can today send their children to multiracial schools, and they do have access to world-class health facilities that were previously reserved for white people in their suburbs. The black children who were born in formerly white residential areas relate to apartheid through history textbooks at school; their daily reality *is* that of a racially integrated society. To these children, the idea of white superiority does not make sense because there is nothing that white children do that they themselves do not do.

While members of the black elite may still complain about subtle forms of racial discrimination in the workplace, it is true that the new political order in South Africa has transformed and made industrial relations much better for the black elite. Under apartheid, the idea of a black manager supervising a white person was anathema. While the corporate world is still dominated by white people, black professionals today do occupy senior positions that they could never have hoped to occupy under apartheid.

Even in such deeply social areas as the realm of love, 1994 has deconstructed the racial restrictions that were put in place by the social engineers of apartheid. Few as inter-racial marriages evidently are, they are no longer an impossibility guaranteed by law. South Africans who are driven in adventurous directions by their feelings do fall in love and marry across the colour line. Of course, this is not an area where transformation can be fast-tracked mechanically through legislative instruments; matters of love are deeply personal and are influenced by a complexity of socio-cultural factors that have no respect for legal dec-larations. This is the area of life where the liberal principle of individual choice has the widest leeway.

Whatever the positive shifts we have experienced in social relations, there still remains a major challenge in the way in which individu-als perceive each other through the prism of race thinking. Further, race-based inequalities expressed in, amongst others, the differential material endowment of the white and black race in South Africa today clearly suggest the ANC government has a long way to go in overhaul-ing the offshoots of the previous order.

Crucially, the social existence of different races in South Africa con-tinues, by and large, to be within the spatial planning framework of the apartheid system. This has not been altered in any fundamental way. The ANC has failed in its objective to 'overcome the legacy of inequali-ty and injustice created by colonialism and apartheid'.[4] Asset ownership in the form of titled houses, investments in the stock market, owner-ship of intellectual property and ownership of businesses remain over-whelmingly white, a path continuation from the massive injection of legally enforced privileges under apartheid. The social transformation that has taken place in South Africa since 1994 has actually reinforced inequality and sustained the status quo, with little changes here and there. It has been an elitist process, empowering a few members of the black elite and narrowing the income and wealth gap between them and their white counterparts.

While the members of the black elite have climbed the economic ladder, the vast majority of the black poor remain at the bottom of the economic system. The bulk of the unemployed in South Africa are black, with unemployment amongst whites comparably lower. According to academics Ashraf Kariem and Sithembile Mbete, in 2009, 53.4% of black African youth between the ages of 15 and 24 were unemployed, compared to 14.5% of white youth – a reality that amplifies the legacy of the apartheid past and poor management of the education system by the ANC government.[5] Similarly, whites continue to dominate the managerial echelons of the corporate sector.

While there are many explanations for the failure of the ANC to bridge the inequality gap, the under-performance of the public education system is among the most important drivers of inequality. The few blacks who managed to take advantage of the economic opportunities presented by conditions of freedom after 1994 were enabled by education. It is equally true that the millions of young blacks who have been swelling the ranks of the unemployed since the dawn of democracy are victims of a dysfunctional public education system. The greatest crime committed by the ANC government against black people has been the maiming of the future of millions of black children. How are we to explain the fact that, every year, an average of 300 000 pupils who pass matric neither proceed to higher education nor find work?

The social consequences of a failing education system can be underestimated only by people who do not appreciate the importance of education in social change. A child from a poor black family who has been rescued from poverty by education represents a generational breaking point between the penury of his or her parents and the real prospects of a future generation of middle-class or well-off grandchildren. Similarly, a black child who is dumped into the reservoir of the unemployed by a dysfunctional education system is an ingredient for the reproduction of mass poverty among black people. The socio-economic progress of societies depends on the effectiveness of their public education systems. Unfortunately, this is where the ANC has failed South Africans.

The dictatorship of money

The social investment of the ANC-led government notwithstanding, the first two decades of democracy can be characterised as the 'dictatorship of money'. Harvard historian Niall Ferguson studied the history of money:

> Bread, cash, dosh, dough, lucre, moolah, the wherewithal: call it what you like, money matters. To Christians, the love of it is the root of all evil. To generals, it is the sinews of war; to revolutionaries, the shackles of labour.[6]

What Ferguson does not say is that Christians, generals, revolutionaries and comrades want money. They may claim not to love it, but they all want it.

In post-apartheid South Africa, money overtook politics as the real liberator. The hope of the masses of black people that political freedom would deliver economic miracles turned out to be a utopian dream. Only money delivered miracles to the people who have been fortunate to have it. When all things are said and done, it is moneyed people who have witnessed the paradise of democracy in South Africa.

Ironically, money has not discriminated against whites in delivering its economic miracles. White people with money have not only enjoyed good lives, but they have made more money in democratic South Africa. And, through money, they have been able to insulate themselves from the general collapse of public services. When they lost confidence in the public service, they found refuge in the private sector, which has grown tremendously since 1994, ever developing the capacity to provide almost all the services that are traditionally associated with the state. The truth about post-apartheid South Africa is that, if you have money, you can literally do without the state. You can send your children to a private school, have your sick parents treated in a private hospital, or use private security to protect your house.

Money has also served as the great racial unifier; it brought a few black people into the economic paradise previously enjoyed by whites only. As soon as a black person acquired money, he or she relocated quickly from a township to one of the formerly white suburbs, where money reigns supreme. Through money, the black elite suddenly gained access to the comfortable life of the city, living side by side with white people who had been assisted by apartheid to monopolise the 'good' life in town. Essentially, the rainbow communities of our towns are money communities. Where there is no money, there are no rainbow communities. The reason poor black and white people do not live together in the same communities is that they do not have money. Wherever white and black people live together there is money.

Money has also transformed the social character of our towns and cities. There was a time when city centres used to be the place for all to go shopping. Nowadays, because of money, rich people have built shopping malls for themselves. They have left behind decaying inner cities to the poor, who are mainly black people. When they realised that taxis were increasingly enabling the poor to reach malls in the suburbs, the rich began building tailored malls for township dwellers, so that the spaces between the rich and poor did not meet. The rich do not like mingling with the poor.

All these developments were facilitated by money; they were not engineered by the ANC. The ANC has little power to control social dynamics in the meta-state realm. Even if the ANC does not like the phenomenon of high-walled residential estates, it can do nothing to stop its own cadres, acting in their private capacities, from living in them. Where there is freedom people choose what they like, not what is preferred by political parties.

The ANC has itself not escaped the impact of money. Like Ferguson's Christians, generals and revolutionaries, ANC cadres also want money. They, too, want to drive luxury cars. They, too, want to live in mansions.

And they, too, want to enjoy the comforts of the suburbs. This, by the way, is not peculiar to the ANC; it is an old affliction associated with revolutionary parties across the world.

The case of the Communist Party of China is apposite. As soon as it took over state power in 1949, human weaknesses began to reveal themselves among party cadres. City life imposed its decadence upon them:

> *Once in the cities, some veteran cadres immediately strived to enjoy the booty and spoils. They demanded higher positions and more perquisites ... In many of these cases, the officials reprimanded were linked to lavish lifestyles or indecent behaviour such as extramarital affairs, divorcing wives of peasant background to marry young, educated girls ...*[7]

ANC veteran cadres may not be known for extramarital affairs, or for divorcing wives of peasant background to marry educated girls, but they have certainly received perquisites and high positions in government. While this may be viewed as normal and unavoidable, it has had a profoundly negative impact on the party. Under Thabo Mbeki, the word 'careerism' was among the frequently used when decrying alien tendencies that had afflicted the ANC. This was not out of nothing. An observation had been made that seekers of perquisites and high office had infiltrated the ANC to the extent that it was difficult to distinguish a careerist from a genuine cadre.

A perception does exist in South Africa that the ANC is a door to economic opportunities. The ubiquitous cases of corruption involving junior and senior members of the party suggest that there are many among ANC members who view the party as an escape route out of poverty, and a highway to money. If a survey were to be conducted, posing the question 'Is the ANC corrupt?', we think most honest South Africans would probably answer 'Yes'.

The perception of the ANC as a corrupt organisation is fuelled by what people see when they observe the ANC. Meetings of ANC structures increasingly look like luxury car shows. One simply needs to go to a national conference of the ANCYL and observe the expensive cars driven by young ANC cadres for this claim to be brought home. The poor ruralitarians who are brought to, the conferences on buses must wonder which ANC they belong to, that is so indifferent to their own conditions and yet so generous to the cadres who live in the cities. This is how money has transformed the ANC, and indeed our society. Today if you have money, you have power too. Because they have money, the infamous Gupta family could even land a private aircraft full of their relatives and friends at South Africa's military Waterkloof Air Force Base in Pretoria. If you do not have money, you are doomed. This is the truth of our time. The question again arises: is this the kind of society the ANC envisioned?

Chapter 8

THROUGH THE EYE OF IMAGINATION

O bservers of contemporary politics often ask: for how long will the ANC govern South Africa? Delivering his centenary speech on 8 January 2012, ANC president Jacob Zuma said: 'We are determined to move to the second centenary with a more rejuvenated organisation that is strategically positioned to continue to lead the people of our country and continent.' According to Zuma, the people of South Africa and those of the African continent will, for the next century, be led by a strategically positioned ANC – simple and straightforward.

But how does Mr Zuma know that we, the people of Africa and all our grandchildren, will be led by the ANC for the next 100 years? He does not tell us. He seems to believe that, since the ANC has survived for the *past* 100 years, it shall perforce survive for the next century. Given that he made his prophecy at the time when the ANC was a governing party, Zuma could not foresee a reality outside that which existed during his time. History, according to Zuma, is a straight line, reproducing itself in ways that the living can predict.

But Zuma is not the only holder of deterministic notions of history. This is a general tendency among politicians, especially those in power. People who are in power tend to think that they can see the future. They often manufacture prophecies that reproduce their positions of power, prophecies that guarantee a future that continues to be shaped by their past actions.

The logic goes like this: if the ANC is governing today, it shall govern tomorrow. Few politicians in power do not see the future through the prism of their current power. If they could, most politicians would programme the future to replay their song, over and over again.

Since opposition parties are essentially fighting to take over power, they, too, tend to project themselves as the power-in-waiting. History, according to them, is a process towards the dethronement of governing parties and the inauguration of opposition parties as rulers of the new age. This conception is often projected as if it is a natural process. Lindiwe Mazibuko, for example, believes that her party, the Democratic Alliance (DA), is the 'party of the future'.

> … and our [DA] future lies beyond the municipalities of the Western Cape, in which we have made significant inroads in electoral support. With a foothold in government in two other provinces (Gauteng and the Eastern Cape), Johannesburg – and Soweto in particular – symbolises the next frontier for the Democratic Alliance.[1]

In truth, Mazibuko cannot know the future, yet she boldly asserts that the provinces of Gauteng and the Eastern Cape are bridges that will deliver the people of South Africa from her party's provincial power in the Western Cape to a future country wholly governed by the DA. In Mazibuko's mind, therefore, Zuma is a fantasiser, misled by his daydreams into seeing a future that will not happen, a century in which the people of South Africa and those of the African continent are governed by a 'strategically positioned' ANC. Hers is a future led by the DA.

Zuma's and Mazibuko's views are perfect examples of history-making as a contested project. If we believe Zuma, posterity will stand at the end of this century and look back over a historic period shaped by the ANC. But the DA believes the same thing about itself, that *it* will be the party seen by future generations when they seek to retrace their political evolution.

Who, then, are we to believe about the future between the ANC and the DA? The answer is that they are both wrong. No one knows the future. What is helpful is not prophecy, but an explication of the process of social change in order to assist the imagination to grasp possible pictures of the future.

Humankind, an unfolding mystery

People who are grappling with practical problems are prone to confine their imagination within the horizons of their current conditions. Those partaking in the gratification of the moment tend to drown in the sweet waters of pleasure. For these people everything is viewed on the basis of the dictates of today. Given that human beings are rational and hopeful creatures, humanity's general tendency is to expect a better future. Those who have made it in life do not envision a future reversal of their fortunes, and the poor live in the hope that tomorrow will be better.

In a sense, the future is a projection of human aspirations. Our vision of the future is a reflection of the improvements we would like to see in our present conditions. If we visualise a dreadful future, this usually goads us into action to attempt to build a better one. If we think we do not have it within our power to pave our way to a better future, we hope that other people, or something else, will intervene to turn our fortunes. The 'something else' could be friends or relatives, society, government or some higher, supernatural power. What is true of us (rational) human beings is that we always expect an improvement in our lives.

The same principle drives politics. Acting in a political group, human beings retain the driving rationality of progress. This is perfectly understandable, but when it comes to politics it is the very root of subjectivity and delusionary idealism. Even when the odds are clearly against a specific political party, members of that party continue to cling to the idea that the day is coming when they will ascend to power. Some parties eventually disappear in the vanity of their hopes.

The experience of all Black Consciousness parties in South Africa perfectly exemplifies this. All of them have followed a reverse trajectory: from something to nothing. Yet none of them have stopped imagining a better future for themselves. For them, tomorrow always held great promise, but for most of them tomorrow never comes.

While political parties are motivated by their own idealism, history is a social process which inexorably unfolds the essential dynamism of humankind. It does not matter what either the ANC or the DA says about the future. Social change will continue to unfold as if their grand political prophecies were never pronounced, for political parties have little or no control over the mechanics of social change, especially in conditions of political freedom. 'History … when comprehended, shatters the idealistic framework,'[2] as Herbert Marcuse reminds us.

Heroic as it was in the early 1990s, the ANC might have imagined that black children born after 1994 would grow like sheep in the political kraal of the party. But, 20 years down the line, the ANC is concerned about the political flexibility of the so-called born-free generation, the very generation that sprouted out of the freedom to which the ANC contributed.

There was a time in the early days of democracy when the possibility of black South Africans voting for a political party led by a white person would have been inconceivable. There was also a time when the growth of the ANC in KwaZulu-Natal appeared like a mirage. There was a time when the idea that the National Party would ultimately dissolve into the ANC was laughable. But all of these unforeseen developments have come to pass. And, when placed in historical context, they happened within an unbelievably short space of time, almost in a manner that makes predictors of the future appear stupid. Before these things happened, they were not foreseen by the prophets who claimed to possess political foresight.

This is precisely what we mean when we speak of the essential dynamism of humankind. While human beings by nature prefer certainty in the future, they are, as a collective, and indeed as individuals, fundamentally unpredictable. There is something in the essential character of humankind that operates like an ever-unfolding mystery. If political parties appreciated this reality, they would moderate their prophetic pretensions. Perhaps they would be humbler when announcing grand visions about unknown and unknowable futures.

Little things that change society

When we contemplate political change, thought is often directed towards big ideas: big ideologies, big historical events, big leaders. While we cannot downplay the role of 'big' categories in history, the whole picture is imperilled if we do not pay equal attention to the factors which may be less grand but which have also played decisive roles in shaping history.

Karl Popper traces the origins of Western civilisation to little but important things that took place in Greece. While some would like to emphasise the importance of Greek philosophy, this is not what set off the flow of Greek history in the direction of civilisation. As Popper correctly observes, fundamental change in the politics of Ancient Greece was made possible when population growth broke down tribalism as a central organising force in Greek society. Popper explains:

> The breakdown of tribalism, of the closed society of Greece, may be traced to the time when population growth began to make itself felt among the ruling class of the landed proprietors. This meant the end

of 'organic' tribalism. For it created social tension within the closed society of the ruling class.[3]

When imagining the future, the ruling class of Ancient Greece might have thought that the growth of their population would serve to strengthen their position of power, since, in their imagination, a bigger population would imply a bigger power base. But, as Popper observes, the opposite was actually the case. As the population grew, the bonds of tribal authority weakened because more and more subjects could no longer conceive of themselves as belonging to a tribal family tree, ruled by a tribal father figure. People began to question the legitimacy of tribal leaders. As society expanded, it also became more abstract, thus requiring modern instruments of government to hold it together; tribal affinity was no longer effective as an instrument of social cohesion.

This is how a democratic impulse was born in early Greek societies, leading to the development of democracy as a modern system of government. Today it is impossible to speak of democracy without reference to its rudimentary origins in Ancient Greece.

In a modern society, social dynamics do not take as long a period as it took to break down the force of tribalism in Ancient Greece, although the principles driving change may not be fundamentally different. While people may not notice it, the social change that takes place in democratic societies within two decades is ground-breaking. That is the time it takes for a whole new generation of young citizens to make itself felt on the socio-political scene. Two decades do introduce new dynamics into existing political systems.

Let us consider the scenario of social change in post-apartheid South Africa. The children who were born in the year 1990 voted for the first time in the 2009 general elections. There were 3.16 million new voters registered for these elections. There were 20.6 million people registered to vote in the 2004 elections, and 18.1 million for the 1999 elections.

This represents an average voter growth rate of about 2.8 million people per election.

If we project two decades into the future, we can safely assume that, on the basis of past experience, South Africa will, between 2014 and 2034, have added about 11.2 million new voters to its voters' roll. These additions, minus older voters who will exit the system due to death, suggest that the country will have a fundamentally different political picture in the next 20 years, an electoral environment dominated by an overwhelming majority of voters who never experienced apartheid at all.

Every politician who was 55 years old in 2014 will be 75 years old in 2034. Current global social trends point in the direction of a world that is fast losing confidence in old people as drivers of change. From what we are witnessing in world politics today, it does not seem as though future societies will be governed by very old politicians. On the contrary, contemporary societies prefer young leaders – be it in business, civil society or politics. This trend is likely to continue.

These changes will no doubt have profound implications for future societies, including South Africa. Yet the changes will not be occasioned by big ideologies, big historical events or big leaders; they are changes that will arise from the natural dynamism of social evolution – in a way not very different from the breakdown of tribalism in Ancient Greece.

Given current social trends, it would seem that the main issues that drive political discourse in South Africa today – poverty and unemployment, in particular – are most likely to be at the centre of the country's political agenda in the next 20 years, but the debate will in all likelihood shift from apartheid as the bogeyman to the failure of successive post-apartheid governments to improve the socio-economic conditions of the poor.

In 2034 and beyond, the appeal of the liberation struggle as a rallying political call will, in a manner similar to the disappearance of tribalism in Ancient Greece, have lost force. It is worth noting that the year 2034 will mark 40 years of democratic experience in South Africa. A politician who was 30 years old in 2014 will be 50 years old in 2034. There will therefore hardly be a politician in 2034 who would have participated in the liberation struggle. Anyone making reference to the liberation struggle would essentially be referring to what departed people had done. Reference to the struggle will sound like dead history, buried in textbooks, with little practical relevance to the problems of the living.

The 'God help us' scenario

Society in the next 20 years is likely to reflect a magnified picture of the macro-social trends that already characterise South Africa today. It is a society defined by acute economic inequality, where whites are better off compared to blacks, but where this reality is eclipsed by a socially visible black middle class that enjoys the same economic privileges enjoyed by their white counterparts.

The social and economic linkages between whites and the black elite will further eclipse race as a dividing social line. The social outcomes of 40 years of racial mingling among whites and members of the black elite will have produced more inter-racial marital partnerships. It will no longer be a curiosity to encounter mixed couples in the shopping malls of tomorrow. But this will still be confined to the middle class or more affluent sections of society. The future prospects of deepening social relations between poor white and black people are slim. The socio-spatial gulf that separates these poor people is reproduced by lack of money. Unlike well-off black people, poor blacks do not enjoy the freedom of social mobility.

The divide between the haves and the have-nots will still be mediated by the old apartheid spatial planning that has locked up millions of poor blacks in townships. Prime suburbs will still be the exclusive preserve of a rich, racially diluted minority, although informal settlements of the poor are likely to encroach more and more into urban spaces, much to the discomfort of the elite – black and white. The phenomenon of high-wall security residential estates will be more visible in all our towns and cities. City dwellers will continue to migrate from traditional stand-alone houses into gated 24-hour security estates. As Terry Eagleton correctly observes: 'It is not hard to imagine affluent communities of the future protected by watchtowers, searchlights and machine guns, while the poor scavenge for food in the wastelands beyond.'[4] In South Africa, this is already happening. What we do not know is how fast the trend will develop. We also do not know how long it will take before the poor go on a rampage, breaking and looting the mansions of rich people in the suburbs for food.

The private sector will be the most preferred supplier of social services such as education, health care, security, and so on. Even among the poor, private institutions will likely mushroom to provide traditionally public services. The state might even be weaker, driven by a predatory elite, using the state essentially as an instrument of private accumulation. In such a scenario, politicians will not be trusted by the people, but politicians will not stop claiming to be tribunes of the people. In such a scenario, a great deal of cynicism will attach to politics. There will be a rise of messianic politics – a politics characterised by weak public institutions, dominated by theatrical individuals who pretend to be the hope of the people. 'I am the only hope for South Africa,' the messiahs of tomorrow will claim.

Public institutions will be so delegitimised that citizens will have no faith in them. Corruption will be so rampant and entrenched that public noise against it will inspire no hope. People will know that everyone in government is corrupt: from the president to the municipal official. The small guy will from time to time be punished in order for him to serve as an example that government is 'committed' to fighting corruption, but the big guys will not go to jail. Only the politicians who are on the wrong side of factional politics will be tormented by security agencies. The case of Julius Malema and Jacob Zuma is likely to serve as a future template. Those in power will pursue their political enemies, but the public will know that the cat is as dirty as the mouse.

A society like this will be sustained by a dysfunctional public education system, driven by politicians who pay lip service to quality education. This will be made possible by the availability of an alternative, private education for the children of the elite. The elite will still make moralistic noises about the importance of public education, but their children will go to good schools in town. There will be a growing number of teachers in township and rural schools who send their children to schools in town, a clear sign that the teachers have little confidence in the quality of the teaching they deliver.

Driven by a quick-fix mentality and over-zealousness to produce glossy results, politicians will dupe the public by doctoring improvements in matric results, but the results will be based on ridiculously low standards. The national tragedy, though, will be that while the children of the elite will be insulated from this mediocre public education, private education will not be able to meet the demands of a skills-hungry and modernisation-needy economy. This situation will feed and reproduce inequality.

Most of the goods consumed by South Africans will be imports from China, South Korea, India and other parts of the world. Yet South African politicians will not stop mouthing slogans of national greatness, while international observers laugh at us. International reliance on mineral resources from South Africa will diminish, owing to investor distrust of the ability of the South African government to maintain order and economic stability. The rand will resemble a yo-yo, swinging up and down whenever investors feel restless. Increasingly, wealthier South Africans will open private offshore bank accounts, hoping to protect their money from perennial domestic uncertainty. Investment anxiety will be the order of the day. Capital flight is a real possibility.

In this scenario, the poor will not lie dormant; they will from time to time wage violent protests. When such protests erupt, politicians will not have the courage to go to address rampaging mobs because they will have lost touch with the masses. The situation will be left to security forces, who will have to kill a few or many protesters each time there is a confrontation. Nobody will call for the institution of a commission of inquiry after such skirmishes, as the general image of commissions of inquiry will have been sullied by the inaction of politicians following their recommendations. Or commissions of inquiry will be perceived as instruments used by politicians to shield themselves from culpability.

This scenario is nasty and undesirable, but current trends point in this direction. The scenario will be possible if the political environment continues to be dominated by the ANC, with no prospects of political change. If the ANC governs until 2034 and beyond, the hope for political change will be dashed by the arrogance of a party that would have been in power for more than 40 years. By then anyone who suggests that change is possible would look like a madman. Opportunistic citizens who view politics as a gateway to economic success will join the ANC, knowing that they are guaranteed rewarding positions in the state. People will be dissuaded from opposition politics, since the past 40 years would have proven opposition politics futile. There would be fewer opposition parties, and probably one main opposition party such as the DA. Opposition politics would be the domain of a few self-appointed angels, making noise in a political environment where kleptocrats reign supreme.

Under such circumstances, the ANC is likely to become a mafia organisation, controlled by cliques, factions, gangs and tribal entrepreneurs. Cadres will be at large at dusk, clad in balaclavas, and will be feigning seriousness in a branch or NEC meeting during the day. Well-meaning leaders of the ANC will be among the most frustrated in society, feeling helpless within a party that has been hijacked by swindlers.

But these 'well-meaning' leaders will be scared to leave the party, fearing hunger outside the patronage network of the ANC.

'It is cold out there,' concerned leaders will be warned by those who once attempted unsuccessfully to break out of the ANC, such as the Congress of the People (COPE) and the Economic Freedom Fighters (EFF). The failed experiments of the past 40 years – such as Agang SA – would also be a big demotivation for political experimentalism.

We call this a 'God help us' scenario. Many would pray that we never get there. But it is not impossible.

Towards the ideal

A different scenario is also possible. The ideal society would in many ways reflect a trajectory different from the 'God help us' scenario, but it would not be its direct opposite. Neither would it be a perfect scenario. We do not believe that South Africa will one day be a 'perfect' society. Indeed, we do not know of a perfect society in the world. But South Africa can be steered away from hopelessness. The country can be better.

Society is a complex, formless organism. It does not move in leaps and bounds. Mao Zedong had a warped conception of society. He thought it could be caused to make a Great Leap Forward. This was idealism at its worst, and it was bound to fail. It is true that Mao's successors, particularly Deng Xiaoping, have improved socio-economic conditions in China, but it has been a slow, steady process, not a Great Leap Forward.

South Africa's road to an ideal society would be similar. It would take incremental actions, over a period of time, to make this country better. We won't wake up one day to a better country today that was a mess yesterday.

As we will observe below, the success of modern societies largely mirrors the effectiveness of their public education systems. It is impossible for South Africa to progress towards an ideal society without a fundamental turnaround of the country's public education system. For as long as excellence is associated with private schools and not public ones, we can be assured that our country will drift in the wrong direction.

It is public education that can produce the skills required by our economy. This can be achieved only if our schools are turned around to produce learners who are ready to advance to a higher education system geared for a modern economy. There also needs to be a seamless transition between school and higher education institutions. The current situation in which masses of pupils who pass matric do not proceed to higher education is a road to social disaster. In fact, our current public education system is a factory for social dysfunction. The irony of the system is that while our economy is skills hungry, the education system produces masses of young adults who are poorly educated and irrelevant to the economy.

A turnaround in the system would entail fixing our schools by providing support for principals to better manage them, and to get communities more involved in monitoring school performance. Principals and teachers must be made to account to local communities when schools are not performing, and government must be pressured to take drastic action against non-performing schools.

Our public education system must also be reclaimed from the destructive control of unions. The children who are in the schools are not the children of unionists; they are the sons and daughters of ordinary parents who want their children to succeed. These children are our national assets. We cannot allow their future to be held to ransom by selfish union leaders and rogue elements. If our education system is not unshackled from disruptive unionism, an ideal society will remain a chimera.

Our higher education system also needs a serious overhaul. The long, chaotic admission queues at the beginning of the year at our universities are a sign of a higher education system without the capacity to absorb a greater number of students. The idea of Further Education and Training (FET) colleges is sound, for our economy requires as many artisans as it requires theoreticians. But the quality of the education delivered at these institutions does not inspire the confidence of parents whose children have done well in matric. It must be remembered that for most students in higher education, what matters most is the prospect of employment upon completion of their studies.

The perception that the graduates from FET colleges struggle more than those from universities to find jobs must be addressed by demonstrating practically that this will in future not be the case. In short, our higher education system requires improvements in quality as well as in widening access.

There should be no reason why an education system cannot be overhauled within a 20-year period. Failure to do this would mean squandering the future of whole generations of South Africans. It would mean postponing the development of the country by more than two decades. This is what the ANC-led government has done in the first two decades of democracy; it has failed to produce a critical mass of highly skilled South Africans to propel an economic revolution. Even during boom years, between 2000 and 2007, the country failed to take advantage of favourable global economic conditions, due to acute skills shortages.

Our point is that South Africa will only move closer to an ideal society the day it is characterised by a well-educated and skilled citizenry that is able to take advantage of the opportunities presented by a modern economy. It must also be a citizenry inspired by education to explore new ideas which can lead to the setting up of new factories to produce a whole range of commodities required by modern societies. In the same way that we buy goods manufactured in South Korea, the rest of the world should consume goods produced by South African citizens. This is the only way to economic prosperity in tomorrow's highly competitive global economic environment.

The citizenry of an ideal South African society would be economically independent, socially engaged and politically flexible. It would be economically independent in the sense that it would not depend on the state for its livelihood; it would derive incomes from professional jobs and economic initiatives related to its training. Such a citizenry would be socially engaged in that its economic independence would deal a fatal blow to the dormancy that usually attaches to state dependency. It would be politically flexible in the sense that its education would empower it with the audacity and capacity critically and freely, without fear of repercussions, to evaluate available political alternatives.

Such a critical citizenry would be good for the general health of democracy. Politicians would be kept on their toes, always mindful of the potential consequences of complacency. A socially engaged citizenry would demand better services and insist on higher standards in the management of public institutions which are sustained by the taxpayer's money. A politically flexible citizenry would not hesitate to shift political allegiance as soon as a governing party messes up. The blackmail of liberation heroism would not be enough to sustain the allegiance of an informed electorate.

How, then, would such a citizenry impact on our politics? The first possibility would be a fundamental transformation of the ANC, from its current state of arrogance and complacency to a more accountable party that is fearful of the real possibility of losing power. This would be good for the long-term sustainability of the ANC in that it would be imbued with the capacity for continuous self-renewal, driven by the expectations of the electorate. This would cleanse the party of its current impurities – of corruption and incompetent leadership in all three spheres of government. In a way, the ANC would have to undergo some kind of rebirth – first dying as a party ill-suited for a modern society, and then being reborn as a party sensitive to the demands of a politically flexible electorate.

Corruptible leaders like Jacob Zuma would be kicked out of the party because they would be a liability. If the ANC did not act against such rogue elements, the electorate would kick the party out of power, leading to the second possibility outlined hereunder. Are we going to witness this by 2034? No one knows, but it is not impossible.

The second possibility would be the rise of the DA, benefiting from the self-inflicted death of the ANC. But, as we point out in the next chapter, the DA would be unlikely to take advantage of the political space left by the ANC, if it clung to its fundamental character as a party for whites. The party would have to be African-led if it were to appeal to the majority of the country's population. For the purposes of nation building, the party would need to maintain an inclusive internal political culture so that minorities do not feel repelled from the party. Space would need to be reserved for whites also to hold positions of leadership in the party to avert complaints of excessive Africanisation. Will the DA ever demonstrate this kind of courage? No one knows, but it is not impossible.

The last possibility would be what various politicians have been trying to do over the past 20 years – attempt to introduce a new political party, positioned as a credible alternative to the ANC. This would have two dimensions: either a party led and dominated by former leaders and members of the ANC, or a party led and dominated by people who were not members of the ANC, even if they may have been voting for the ANC. Such people would be black, and weary of the DA, although not repellent to white South Africans.

As easy as this possibility may appear, it would be very difficult to maintain its coherence, for it takes time to build long-lasting political parties. Furthermore, parties that come from the ANC always face the danger of reproducing ANC weaknesses, such as factionalism and corruption. Will we finally witness the success of what various politicians have been trying and failing to do? No one knows, but it is not impossible.

Whatever we may think, the tendency to imagine the future as if South Africa is a static country is not helpful. To imagine that the political passions of today will not change and that the attachment of most South Africans to liberation politics will remain the same, even at a time when there will be no leader who would have participated in the liberation struggle in 2034, seems unrealistic.

To the unimaginative, the scenarios we have highlighted in this book may appear far-fetched, but, as we have suggested, no one knows the future. Those who will be fortunate enough to live and witness the year 2034 will pull this book from their shelves to check if, in 2014, we were hallucinating or engaged in serious prognostic work. If it turns out that we were wrong, and if we, too, are still alive 20 years from now, we will be humble enough to eat our own socks.

Chapter 9

WILL CHANGE IMPOSE ITSELF?

What will it take for South Africa to experiment with a different politics? If the ANC is a spent force, as we believe it is, what should we conceive of in its place? Social change hardly ever happens like a lightning bolt out of the sky; it is often a by-product of human agency. There are men and women who consciously position themselves as change agents across the social and political spheres. Some of their efforts do not amount to much, but some do attain a measure of success.

Those who drive social change do not do so because there are guaranteed outcomes, but out of the understanding that the costs of inaction are dire. Carefully cultivated change yields better outcomes than the hope for some miracle in the distant future. South Africa's democratic breakthrough was a story of courage in the face of the seemingly impossible and mammoth challenge of removing a regime that had been in power for nearly half a century, with its white supremacist philosophy deeply entrenched.

The men and women who took to the streets in protest against the inhumane system of apartheid were ordinary human beings who made a conscious choice to dedicate their lives to a cause. They did so knowing that they might never live to see the fruits of their work, but were inspired by the idea that their lives would count for something for future generations.

There is a universal ring to South Africa's struggle against apartheid. Other nations around the world, particularly on the African continent, in Asia and in South America, had fought to claim the right to define their identity, and to shape the course of their nation's histories. The anti-apartheid struggles, led in the main by the ANC, had an internationalist outlook precisely because its normative language of non-racism, non-sexism, human rights and democracy was a composite part of global struggles against the injustices of colonialism. No nation received its freedom on a platter. Every people that lived under the yoke of oppression had to cast it away either through violent resistance or peaceful protest. Political ideals come at a cost.

The rise of a black middle class in South Africa should be seen as a great promise for democracy, yet this is not the case. While those in power constrain the space for liberty, those who are relatively more empowered to speak forcefully than the rest of society are the most silent. Their material improvement lulls them into a state of false comfort, believing that things will remain the same or improve at some point in the future. They believe that change will impose itself. This is idealism at its worst. In fact, it is disguised escapism.

Change is a process that needs to be driven consciously through innovative civil society initiatives that are of a different shape from those applied in the past, and also through exploring party political alternatives. The key question is: what kind of civil society and alternative political vehicles are required to drive change in South Africa today? However this question is approached, there are certain fundamentals that must be addressed if South Africa is to experience a different kind of politics, a politics cleansed of current impurities.

The first is the need to eliminate the myth of the ANC in the psyche of South African citizens in order to allow for more creative ways of thinking about change beyond the ANC. The second basic step towards change is to ensure a regularity of shifting political allegiances between political parties on the basis of the depth of their leadership, the strength of their values and the quality of their proposed governing programme. Thirdly, there is the need to explore different political alternatives which could potentially be vehicles for political change. Fourthly, we should realise that, at the end of the day, it is ordinary citizens like us who are the ones who can bring about the change we desire. The messianic hope of some kind of saviour somewhere out there may give us opiate feelings now, but it will take us nowhere. We ourselves must act.

Dissolving the myth of the ANC

The success of political parties depends on the extent to which they are able to register their presence in popular psychology. In other words, what do people think when they hear the name of a party being mentioned? If the image that springs to mind is in line with the perception that party strategists prefer, it means the party has succeeded in manufacturing and selling its myth. If people have a negative image about a political party, it means party strategists have failed.

Before they are practical entities, political parties are mythological beings. This is why people ask such questions as: what is the ideology of this party? By asking this, people want to know the mythological character of the party in question.

The ANC, too, is a mythological being. The problem is that it has continued to cling to a frozen African nationalism that is backward looking, and which can no longer offer clear answers to new challenges in South Africa today. It is a nationalism constructed under conditions of oppression, which was an ideology suited for the time when oppression was in force. Since then, the party's book of myths has been kept on the shelf, like a reference book that must not be opened. In the process, the book has gathered dust and younger students are no longer convinced of the relevance of a dusty book of wisdom that is protected from interrogation. The ANC has taken the posture of a hero who, after slaying the dragon on his path, finds himself losing his own compass and being permanently frozen on the same spot, reminiscing about the great victories of the past.

As we have pointed out in the previous chapter, sentimental identification with the ANC on the basis of past memories will at some point disappear. The country's demographics are changing: the 2011 census revealed that about 60% of the population was under the age of 39. For younger South Africans, voting for the ANC for old time's sake will no longer be a determinant of the party's support base, especially as people's conditions are increasingly deteriorating.

The youth born in the 1990s have a different perception of the ANC than the older generation has. Those who may still continue to vote for the party could well be doing so not because they are firmly wedded to its history and memory, but more for perceived lack of political alternatives, and simply following on the path-dependence of their parents who have never voted otherwise.

Already, many young people are fed up with the notion that the ANC holds some divine right to rule forever, as Jacob Zuma likes to dream it will. The youth are more inspired by the possibilities that lie in the future than by fading memories in the distant past. It is from them that we should take a cue and erase the imprisoning mythology of the ANC from our minds. When South Africans are able finally to slay the dragon that is the ANC in their own minds, only then will they fully realise the power that lies within them as their own liberators. As we have discussed in Chapter 3, it is the mythical construct of the ANC as a hero of liberation that has the potency to draw mass appeal. This myth will not last forever.

But we must understand how the myth is sustained. Of all current South African parties, the ANC is still the party that dishes out rhetoric on transformation and is comfortable talking about race-based inequalities. The message of transformation in its multi-layered form that captures race relations, economic participation and exclusion, and inequitable redistribution of opportunities, easily gains traction because race-based inequalities in South Africa today are in your face. This lends the ANC the image of being the only political vehicle that fully grasps the challenges faced by the majority of South Africans, and as the only hope for change in future, even as its message is at the same time undermined by the conspicuous rapaciousness of its leaders.

Young black people who grow up in most townships and rural areas witness a much brighter existence amongst their white peers and the emerging but small black middle class in suburbia. Indeed, an excursion into the metropolis or suburban life of South Africa reveals this in a myriad of ways, not least in relatively better infrastructure, better-equipped public spaces (such as parks and sports clubs), and the population of restaurants by mainly white faces more than black ones – something that is less a reflection of culture than it is of differential economic weight along racial lines. The deconstruction of the mythology of the ANC would have to be accompanied by a practical commitment to alter this state of affairs.

Power to the people, not political elites

Two of the nagging questions that are asked repeatedly in the face of the country's continued political slide are: what needs to be done to turn things around, at least politically? And how can we arrest South Africa's continuing dysfunction under the leadership of the ANC? At a subliminal level, this is an admission of our collective failure to pay attention to active citizenship, which is a critical component of democracy, a theme we address later.

Such questions are also based on the mistaken view that answers lie elsewhere – in external circumstances – or are the preserve of the most gifted and extraordinary, rather than with ordinary people. Big Bang change in society, akin to the revolutions that took place in France in 1789 or the radical overhaul of the Soviet Bloc in 1989, are a black swan – it happens once in many decades. It is in any case not a good thing to wish for such revolutions because they tend to have nasty unintended consequences, such as devouring their own children, in the case of the French Revolution, or the birth of the mafia state in the case of the collapse of the Soviet Bloc. A better life for all has also not come following the Arab Spring. All we see in North Africa is chaos, followed by more chaos. We should certainly not count on having a revolution without blood being spilled, both figuratively and literally.

One of the dangers of expecting a Big Bang change or some external events to break out is that this fosters inertia in the interregnum. In his foreword to Jewish doctor and prisoner of war Miklós Nyiszli's book, *Auschwitz*, Bruno Bettelheim recounts the experiences of prisoners of war in the Nazis' concentration camp. He ponders the complex question: why in Auschwitz did only a few prisoners put up a fight to reclaim their freedom, while many lived a passive existence which they knew would ultimately lead to death – with some marching knowingly to their own deaths in the gas chambers, and with little resistance?[1]

The fact that some chose to take up arms, risk their lives and fight for freedom is, according to Bettelheim, what holds the possibility of restoring our trust in human beings. Bettelheim offers an explanation: a death drive, or losing the will to live for a greater cause, is what makes men's conscience blind to their moral and social responsibilities. That is what is currently at play in South Africa with the mounting corruption, arrogance and abuse of power that is becoming so pervasive in the ruling party. While this is shocking in itself, what should be more shocking is the level of inertia that allows this to continue unabated.

Inertia leads many to ignore the signs of regressive shifts in society. This is when people choose instead to go with the flow in the hope that somehow things may work out favourably for them, or that another (mythical) revolutionary saviour will rescue them. Failure to read the little signs of dysfunction and to adjust one's level of commitment to social change abets the pace of decline.

We have in the past had many people who risked death, left their families to take up arms against the apartheid system and perished in the process, and others who risked going to prison for many years at the cost of not spending time with friends and family. But there were also those who had accepted the fate of existence under apartheid, such as the Bantustan leaders, those who chose to work for the system and be agents of its destructive forces against the liberation struggle; and other ordinary citizens who resigned themselves to passive existence for the sake of self-preservation.

A few who swelled the ranks of the liberation movement and other agencies of resistance distinguished themselves courageously by taking a stand against injustice, even though they knew such an act would cost them their lives. One could say that the inertia of some was at the time understandable, given the brutality of the apartheid security forces and the urge for self-preservation that we as human beings possess in varying degrees. But today, under conditions of relative freedom and with constitutional guarantees, what could possibly explain the passivity that is so widespread in society, especially amongst the black middle class?

In post-1994 South Africa, the black middle class wanted to be able to live as normal citizens rather than as strictly political beings. Understandably so, they wanted to pursue career opportunities and fully to express themselves as consumers. This, too, is an important element of citizenry, as it enables people to make economic choices and enhance their self-esteem as free agents. All of these are fruits of freedom and are reasonable expectations in any democratic society. This, however, is not the totality of the role citizens can play in society; it is also not a complete picture of what one can proudly assert as one's identity. Life has meaning beyond self-preservation or ephemeral comfort. Human beings who have no mission beyond their personal space are as good as non-existent, for their presence has no impact on society.

A view predicated on individualism and self-preservation is based on the misconception of the individual as dis-embedded from society and shielded from the defects that may be induced by either malign neglect or a dysfunctional political leadership. An individual as a totally free entity, unencumbered by moral and social commitments to friends, family and kin, an individual whose own vitality is not dependent on the nourishment offered by social networks and kinship ties, is a libertarian myth that has no foundation in concrete reality.[2] It is unsettling when individuals choose a state of apathy over active engagement.

For its part, the white middle class has chosen to disenfranchise itself politically by making the problem of fixing poor political leadership that of the black middle class, who are supposedly more legitimate to hold a 'black-led' government accountable. This stratum reasons that it has been emasculated by its whiteness, and thus has no legitimacy in the eyes of the ruling elite to assert political views. This pushes its political dialogue to the safe confines of dinner tables with friends or at times to round-table discussions and seminars in small corners. The suggestion that they lack legitimacy is an irrational view based on the unfounded assumption that they need to be legitimated by the ruling elites publicly to express their preference or views about the future of the country. It is also a convenient escape from individual responsibility to whiteness as a delegitimated category which can only exist politically as a victim of the black-led ruling party. Such an irresponsible position of victimhood does not contribute in any meaningful way towards progressive social change.

It is commonplace amongst some sections of the white middle class to express the hope for change in terms of what the black middle class can and should do to force such a change in South Africa. The underlying assumption, of course, is that the white segment of the population is making a silent contribution through paying taxes and contributing skills to rescue the economy – they are the ultimate bulwark against a total slide.

When the white middle class distances itself from the agency of change, its members are abdicating their responsibilities as citizens. They are also conceiving of their role in society in a group sense. In this manner, they are also playing into the disempowering device of the ANC, of treating white South Africans as politically illegitimate and holding them as collectively responsible for the past – a very dubious notion since each individual is responsible for his or her own sins. It is as if the white middle class is politically frozen under an eternal curse cast by the ANC – that the sins of your father shall be visited upon you, up to a thousand generations of those whose skin has a white pigmentation.

We are aware that notions such as black middle class or white middle class are amorphous and do not quite accurately represent individuals or even group self-identity. We use these categories here as a proxy for those who are more materially empowered, those who have some form of higher education qualification, and hold a professional job, or are generally well-to-do. In other words, these categories are important less for their technical rigour than for their convenience in analysing social dynamics.

The point is not so much to proffer a textured analysis of what constitutes the various sub-categories of the middle class, or to evaluate its multifaceted layers, but simply to make the observation that those who make up the bulk of society from whose resources the fiscus is replenished are better positioned to take a strong stand against the ANC's corruption. They are also in a privileged space to start up social causes that may generate a better quality of life for those who are marginalised. They can use their skills, capabilities and voices to empower the less empowered. This is different from the limited and disempowering view of leadership as something that others – mostly politicians – should exercise. Since the middle classes have ceded power to politicians, they have become powerless by choice.

While we may have in a formal sense gained freedom, we fail to realise such freedom in a positive sense to improve the quality of our governance by holding authorities to account, or engaging actively in civic
processes that are aimed at improving the quality of society or the lot
of those who are economically disempowered. Isaiah Berlin discusses
the notion of negative and positive liberty (or freedom) extensively in
his *Four Essays on Liberty*.[3] The former refers merely to the absence
of man-made obstacles, such as political authority or arbitrary rules
and regulations which actively limit the agency power of individuals or
their ability to advance their interests without violating those of others.

Positive freedom, by contrast, involves conditions within which
individuals can organise their lives. The application of positive freedom is largely in the active exercise of political choices beyond the ballot by taking a clear stand on many social issues. This would include
the type of political arrangement under which individuals may prefer
to live as well as telling those in power that their decisions are wrong or
that their policies represent an obstacle to progress. As citizens in post-
apartheid South Africa, we are yet fully to explore the latter aspect of
our freedom; we have instead allowed the political elites to appropriate
a large chunk of that space. If we hope to change this, we must begin to
think of the people as the real wielders of power.

An unpopular road may lead to heaven

One of the softest, if not safest, forms of protest or of expanding one's
freedom in a democracy is casting a ballot. This gives the voters the
most fulfilling experience of being in touch with and exercising their
power. This has hardly been used optimally, largely because of path-
dependence and a perceived lack of political alternatives. This is where
inertia has been most evident: in the fact that South Africans, by and
large, are stuck in their traditional political affiliations at the ballot.

189

They are not as free as they perceive themselves to be when they cannot make the slightest modification in their electoral behaviour.

Changing voting behaviour does not require permission from anyone else, including the ruling party. It is one way of challenging ourselves internally – realising change within us – as we push for change in the country's political culture and system. Moreover, such a change would also mean that, as citizens, we are more aware of the inherent limits of political parties. But that is a step that needs to begin with us being comfortable in putting a sharp knife into the party we have traditionally supported, and thereby creating a shadow of difference between our identity as free individuals and a ruling party which governs on the basis of borrowed power, but acts like an invincible oligarchy.

When we see ourselves as married to political parties, our capacity to make a strong call for accountability will always be subdued by the party that presents itself as our messiah. Such a distinction is crucial for the health of our democracy in the long run, especially since there is the belief within the ruling party that if you are black and opposed to the ANC you cannot possibly be doing so from the standpoint of individual intellectual freedom. Somehow you are pursuing someone's agenda, presumably a 'white' or counter-revolutionary agenda.

Those who previously were part of the traditional support base of the ANC and who are now unhappy with its conduct in power, but find it difficult to vote differently, are unwittingly strengthening the ANC's grip on power and reinforcing its chaotic governance. Many who through their mouths oppose the ANC but at the ballot continue to vote for it argue that there is no alternative, yet they have barely challenged themselves in the act of simply voting differently as a self-empowering step. It is not entirely honest to suggest that there is no alternative when no other party apart from the ANC, post-apartheid, has been *given* an opportunity to govern the country.

Opposition politics is generally seen as a lost cause by those who regard politics as a realm of fate. English journalist and lay theologian Gilbert K. Chesterton warns us not to completely throw away those avenues for change that have been rejected by sections of humankind as lost causes. He notes:

> *The task of modern idealists indeed is made much too easy for them by the fact that they are always taught that if a thing has been defeated it has been disproved ... [But] the lost causes are exactly those which might have saved the world.*[4]

It is the lost causes of opposition or alternative parties that we should be cultivating more as an antidote to the grip of the ANC in our psyche. The question, then, is: where to from here?

Immediate choices we must make

While some, out of inertia, are adjusting to the pseudo-permanency of the myth of the ANC leadership – that is, that it will rule until the return of Jesus Christ – it is important to keep faith in human agency, in particular the ability of human beings to push for progressive change beyond the liberation movement. Even as we think about future political possibilities that could replace the ANC, we should not lose sight of the fact that having a different political party will not suddenly dissolve the complex problems in our economy, social inequalities and unemployment. It may just help us to build a better institutional framework which could in the long run enable us to lay the building blocks of a better society.

There will always be anxieties about socio-economic challenges or the resilience of our institutions, but we need to get to the point where there is at least some shared understanding of what, at the minimum level, it should take to achieve social and economic stability; and what it means to be a winning nation. Constantly searching for possible political alternatives to managing change is but one avenue. Accordingly, there are four political options that confront us today, especially in the wake of the emergence of Agang SA, founded by Mamphela Ramphele, and the newest kid on the block – the Economic Freedom Fighters (EFF), founded by Julius Malema.

The first option is to live with the status quo, which is ANC rule, and continue to hope that it will cleanse itself of its glaring impurities, finally come to its senses, and lead us to the political Utopia envisaged by its nebulous National Democratic Revolution. Its leaders have been exhorting us to be patient with the party because it will, like a river, cleanse itself and effect some organisational renewal that would ensure the restoration of its credible leadership in society.

The problem with this option is the fact that the ANC is a poisoned river that has been slowly killing off the best of its talent. It is a magnet for political riff-raff and cadres who lust after tenders and those who, learning from its president, Jacob Zuma, seek to turn the state into an avenue for personal gain. As we have asserted in this book, it is our belief that the ANC is technically dead and incapable of renewing itself. It is a front organisation for Zuma's acolytes and those whose business is thieving. This party is exactly what we need to transcend, to kill in our psyche, if we are to build anew. Turning our backs on the ANC would be an affirmation of faith in our ability to drive change without the mediation of a party oligarchy that is out of touch with society.

The second possibility presents itself in the shape of the DA. There is a clear indication that the DA is investing energies in its young and upcoming black leaders with a view to elevating their profile in the party. In this sense the DA shows signs of agility and has a solid organisational infrastructure. Its gradual rise could see the party notching hefty electoral gains in 2019 on the back of disgruntlement with the ANC, and the appeal of its brand of leadership to an increasing electorate of younger people. In future, young people may identify more closely with Lindiwe Mazibuko and Mmusi Maimane than they would with Gwede Mantashe or Blade Nzimande. The DA's diverse support base may already be portraying a party on the rise to extending its electoral base.

It is possible, too, that the DA's climb may already be peaking. It is inconceivable that the party will eventually become a juggernaut that crushes the ANC at the polls. There is a significant section of the majority of blacks which just does not trust the DA. They see it as a fragment of the past white rule in South Africa. This race-based antipathy to the DA runs deep, even amongst those who are dissatisfied with the current state of the ANC. They dismiss the notion of the DA's rise mischievously as a back-door return of white rule in South Africa.

Of late, the DA seems to be learning all the wrong things from the ANC. First, it waged a futile battle over the ownership of the struggle legacy with the ANC. The memory of the past is what the ANC thrives on, and it is therefore unclear why the DA chose to go in this direction when it could have been spending more time painting the canvas of the future. Second, it took pragmatism too far by receiving into its fold the Thembu king Buyelekhaya Dalindyebo despite his chequered record and public admission that he breaks the law by smoking dagga. While Dalindyebo fits the image of an ANC cadre perfectly, he seems quite out of place in the DA, a sign of things to come in the party.

Critically, there does not seem to be meaningful conversations within the DA on issues of race and socio-economic cohesiveness. The party has opted for ambiguity on questions of race. It has no well-articulated philosophical view for dealing with this lest it offends its core constituency. Instead, the DA resorts to standard philosophical explanations, leaning on liberalism and placing emphasis on the partially developed notion of an equal-opportunity society, without a serious attempt at identifying the root causes of inequalities in the first place, and then to address them vigorously at the core. This is made trickier by the strong association of social inequalities with the politics of race, even in the light of the growing middle class.

The DA leaves answers to socio-economic inequalities to the trickle-down effects of GDP growth, according to which a growing aggregate output leads to a levelling of social inequalities. Essentially, the party has failed to hone a genuine transformational narrative that connects the aspirations of black communities and expectations of the well-off in the Western Cape. The party does not need to adopt the ANC's or any populist thesis on race, but it should have a deep internal conversation about it. The leadership of the party, throughout the country, must also change to reflect the reality that South Africa is an African country, not a European outpost in Africa.

Moreover, the DA should evolve its own philosophy, which it can present more fluently and credibly and with more substance than anything we have had in the past. Being transformational does not mean looking more like the ANC; it entails taking the necessary steps to connect deeply with social reality from the standpoint of legitimate social purpose, principle and a broadly supported governing programme. In addition, to establish solid legitimacy, the party would need to go beyond finesse in public administration and showcase a better picture of the future in the province it currently runs. Such a future must include all South Africans – black and white. This must not be misconstrued to mean that the DA should be so desperate as to swell its ranks with convicted criminals or self-confessed dagga smokers like King Dalindyebo – simply because the criminals are black. The party must not attempt to out-compete the ANC by styling itself as a friendlier home for criminals.

The notion of an equal-opportunity society promoted by the DA ignores the current realities of race-based inequalities; it anaesthetises the serious issues facing the country by making a false leap to a post-racial Utopia. Making a case for an equal-opportunity society, though credible and worthy, needs a concrete pillar that facilitates redress and economic redistribution along the axis of race-based disadvantages. It is not just the lack of a framework of equality of opportunity that is a problem, a point selectively argued by the DA in its various policy documents, including its 2012 growth strategy, but the fact that there is insufficient attention paid to addressing the conditions that gave rise to uneven access to opportunities in the first place.

The third immediate choice is presented by the launch of a new political party, Agang SA. The problem is that, so far, there is no serious leadership core beyond Dr Mamphela Ramphele to allow for a fair assessment of the prospects of this party. The team she has announced does not inspire confidence. If the people she has presented are known, they must be known in some obscure boardrooms, not in South African politics. Frankly, Agang SA has the appearance of a one-woman-show: Ramphele. However gifted, it is impossible for one person to register a presence nationally. People want to feel the presence of a party in their own neighbourhood; they do not want to relate to a political party through newspaper articles or television. Importantly, one-man or one-woman parties have not done well in South Africa historically. There is a critical question that voters ask: beyond the leader – Ramphele – who else do we know?

This question applies to Bantu Holomisa. It applies to Themba Godi of the African People's Convention, to Kenneth Meshoe of the African Christian Democratic Party, and to Zanele Magwaza-Msibi of the National Freedom Party. Patricia de Lille could not answer the same question before she was swallowed up into the DA.

Respected as she may be in upper-class circles, Ramphele is old. Five years from now, she can no longer inspire those who hope to build the future of this country. In our view, she will be very much the face of the past or become a political nonentity. The imagination of the future beyond Ramphele has to be assisted by the prominent presence of inspirational younger leaders who, from the outset, are poised clearly to take over the baton – otherwise, people will instinctively doubt the sustainability of Agang SA as a political party of the future.

A new political party must never arouse doubt. It must look like a real party of today and tomorrow. Agang SA has not done this. It has only generated an elite storm that holds no promise for thoroughgoing social change.

Beyond its less than-impressive-launch, Agang SA has disappeared into the realm of speculation. The little that has been circulated in the public domain leaves discerning voters asking the question: what is new? Agang SA's policies are couched in high-sounding generalities. They can only appeal to those who harbour philosophical pretensions. For a poor voter in an informal settlement, the party's obsession with the changing of electoral laws only induces confusion. There is a gap between the party's high-sounding sophistry and the concrete aspirations of ordinary South Africans.

There is a general tendency for politicians to over-blow their own importance, thinking that their magnified personalities will automatically translate into mass appeal. Circulating among the chartering classes can easily balloon the head of a leader, and cause him (or her) to forget that a buzz among high-flyers does not often reach the underclass. A household name in suburbia may not be so well-known in the informal settlements of our country, and it is in the latter where the masses of voters reside. Will Dr Mamphela Ramphele pass this litmus test?

The last option is the newest: the EFF of the expelled ANCYL president Julius Malema. From the day it was launched, Malema's party appeared like a band of mad young men, harbouring uncontainable rage against their former leader, Jacob Zuma. Their ideological positioning is on the extreme side of the left – far more left than the increasingly irrelevant SACP. The EFF ideology is enmeshed with a mad version of Africanism, akin to that of Robert Mugabe which has impoverished masses of Zimbabweans. Malema and his fellow travellers hope to nationalise mines and grab land from white owners without compensation. This, they claim, will be done in the interests of poor black people.

Unlike Agang SA, the EFF cannot be accused of obscurity with regard to its policy orientation. In its July 2013 national assembly, the party adopted several policy positions. These include land expropriation and redistribution without compensation, and the nationalisation of mines, banks and other strategic sectors of the economy. This radical policy stance appeals to a specific constituency in South Africa.

Given the youth of Malema and his EFF comrades, it is not surprising that their party is targeting the youth. The fact that South Africa has a large reservoir of unemployed young people positions the EFF better to take advantage of the conditions of the jobless youth. Malema must not be underestimated; he can do better than Ramphele and other small opposition parties electorally. Desperation clouds judgement. The masses of disparate South African youth are vulnerable to all manner of scoundrels.

Frankly, the EFF is a very dangerous party for South Africa. It is a band of anarchists who seem prepared to tear the country apart. If this group were to be given political power, the country would be plunged into chaos. There would be an investment stampede out of South Africa by both foreign and domestic investors fearing for the safety of their money. Who would invest their money in a country constantly under the menace of nationalisation?

The rand would collapse like the Zimbabwean dollar. And we could comically end up using the currency of the same imperialists Malema hates – the Americans. Anyone who thinks this is scaremongering must look north of the Limpopo. Mugabe hates the Americans with all his heart, but he uses their currency to buy the food he eats every day. This is the irony of the so-called revolution in Zimbabwe. Very soon, if the EFF were to gain power, the same could very easily be South Africa's irony too.

The fact that the leader of the EFF has been in trouble with the law casts a shadow of criminality over the party. In the same way that Jacob Zuma has been ducking and diving the law, Julius Malema can easily be perceived as someone who started a party in order to mobilise mobs to go and chant outside our courts of law whenever he (Malema) makes an appearance. In a strange way, Malema and Zuma seem to be united by the fugitive character of their politics.

Whatever South Africans choose, they must be prepared to live with the consequences of their choice. What is clear, though, is that the complexities of the country's politics require that any party that hopes seriously to challenge the ANC must position itself closer to the socially marginalised, including developing a view on race, championing issues of social justice, and maintaining a tight balance between social and economic inclusion on the one hand, and market-based economics on the other.

Leave ancestors in their graves

There are many who believe that our political problems today are due to the absence of leaders such as Robert Sobukwe, Albert Luthuli, Joe Slovo, Oliver Tambo, Steve Biko, Nelson Mandela or their equivalents. Success is viewed as a function of reinventing such leaders today. It is not only the ANC that is entranced by the idealism of the past. A significant portion of South Africa's society yearns for a mythical golden age, when leaders were truly leaders, unsullied by human fallibility. For the ANC, this mythology of leadership, in accord with its own liberation narrative, serves to bolster its image as the only party that can breed leaders for our country.

The danger with fixation upon the mythical golden age is that this only fuels our inertia. It makes us feel powerless in comparison with what must have been the unflagging spirit of the departed heroes. If we could only have their potion of power, all would be well – or so it is reasoned. Instead we should recognise that theirs was a human effort, but also that we are capable of emulating their human effort for the specific challenges that confront us today. The fact that we feel perplexed at the moment is no sign that we do not have what it takes to change our political and social conditions, and play a meaningful part in shaping a better future for the next generation.

Each generation has a set of its own challenges. It must carry its own burdens and negotiate its own treacherous waters into the future. Similarly, every leader emerging from within a generation has his or her mission intricately bound up with the challenges of that particular generation. Such a leader might, in the process of executing his or her tasks, leave an echo that reverberates into the future. As much as present leaders cannot transport themselves back into the past, so are past leaders limited in their influence over the present and the future.

To wish that we had the leaders of yesterday leading us today is missing an important point, namely, that there are no leaders more attuned and better suited to deal with our realities than those we can find among the living today. Wisdom is not restricted to the dead. The ANC believes in the power of its ancestors, for it has contented itself with being the party of the past. It is indeed the party whose spirit is dead. But it is from within our generation that capable leaders who can take the country forward will be found.

Liberation movement heroes operated in conditions that were vastly different to those we are confronted with today. They had a clearly defined enemy that was expressed in the elaborate and diabolical system of apartheid. Their primary role was not to fix things, but to bring about the downfall of apartheid. What we face today are complex challenges of rethinking what it means to be a new nation, to coexist healthily as different races, and to fix governance. This was the ANC's job in hand, and it is what the party is failing to do. It is possible that were leaders such as Tambo, Sobukwe and Biko still alive today, they might not necessarily have created miracles, but might have become part of the problem themselves.

The African continent has many examples of liberation heroes who transformed more or less overnight into enemies of progress. While the values embodied by our freedom fighters are timeless and transcend race and nationality, there is nothing extraordinary about them that the current generation cannot express in exceedingly greater measure. The seed of leadership is planted in every generation, and it is up to each generation in turn to nurture it. What the country needs urgently, and that should emerge from within this generation, are leaders who are able to negotiate the difficult tensions that still mark our transition from the apartheid past.

Leaders should be able to create a space where trust and understanding can be nurtured, as well as to build, through dialogue, enduring bridges towards a shared destiny. We should not narrow our focus in search of leadership only within political parties. Indeed, a new breed of leaders to take the country forward, and that could help nurture and restore integrity in our political system and society, should be found across the different spheres of our society: politics, civil society, the business sector, and a host of other voluntary associations. In short, everyone can be a leader, wherever they are. Thus, we, the people, should not wait for change to come from somewhere far away, to impose itself on us, where we live. This shall not happen.

CONCLUSION

People who might have visited South Africa in 1990 and who returned today would agree that a lot has changed. To a less penetrating mind, the changes that have taken place since 1994 may appear insignificant, for the extraordinary nature of the changes may be eclipsed by the ordinariness of the human beings involved. The people behind the big political changes that took place in South Africa after 1990 were not angels from above, but mere mortals who walked here on Earth. Some of them still live with us today; others have since departed. But what are the ordinary changes that have elevated South Africa into the hallowed category of miracles?

Before 1994, there had not been a black president of the Republic of South Africa. This has been the case since then. Today, in a world where a great deal has happened to alter the centuries-old perception of blackness as sub-human, to say a country in Africa is led by a black president sounds too banal to those searching for profundity. Yet it is true that before 1990, very few white people in South Africa and beyond truly believed that a black man could ever sit in the same chair that used to belong to Prime Minister Hendrik Verwoerd from 1958 to 1966.

The symbolism of a black president is profound. For centuries before 1994, black people in South Africa had been treated like second-class beings. Under the Dutch – from 1652 to 1795 – Africans were viewed as slaves or a nuisance if they occupied land needed by Dutch settlers. Under British colonialism, Africans were converted into labour to service the British-controlled mining industry. Before this, the British also viewed Africans as a nuisance if they occupied land needed by the British to settle the surplus population they imported to South Africa. As we have pointed out in Chapter 1, this is what led to the Frontier Wars.

Under the joint management of South Africa by both the English and the Afrikaner – from 1910 to 1948 – Africans were viewed as surplus population, always available for use in mining, farming or white-owned factories. This essentially remained the same under apartheid, except that the architects of apartheid constructed a much more detailed social system meant to guarantee special privileges for whites and to ensure that, in the social system, blacks did not escape their inferior position.

To people who had lived under these conditions, to see Nelson Mandela being inaugurated as president of South Africa was breathtaking. Suddenly, all the things that white people had been holding as absolute truths about the inferiority of black people evaporated – suddenly a black person was a full human being, and being sworn in to lead a country: South Africa.

Over the past two decades, this change of racial attitude has had to find expression in all spheres of social life. It is no longer taboo for a black man to have a white wife, or a white woman to have a black boyfriend, or a white employee to have a black boss, or a white student to have a black teacher, or a black person to be served by a white waitress at a restaurant. All of these things were illegal before 1994. Today only unreconstructed racists still believe in the so-called sub-humanity of black people. Such racists know that those kinds of beliefs are evil secrets to be hidden in the labyrinths of their hearts of darkness – never to be revealed to the civilised world.

As a liberation movement, and as the party that has been leading South Africa over the past two decades, the ANC has been at the centre of the socio-political changes that have taken place. The party has not been a passive player. It has actively implemented policies that have contributed a great deal to altering the racist social system constructed under colonialism and apartheid.

Since it took over power, the ANC government has built and provided more than 3 million houses free to poor black people; it has provided clean running water to millions of blacks who previously had no access to clean water. It has extended electricity to millions of South Africans who were living in darkness, in forgotten black communities. There is no argument that all these things have helped improve the quality of people's lives. But the story does not end here.

As we have suggested in Chapter 2, the ANC underestimated the extent to which freedom would affect the party. It also overestimated its power to determine change in society. This was a result of a lack of preparedness on the part of the ANC to govern, as well as sheer naivety. There is a temptation liberation movements generally fail to resist: the tendency to view themselves as God Almighty, possessing the power to move mountains.

During the liberation struggle, the ANC had little control over resources. The few resources the ANC had access to were food, military uniforms or money stashed in bags donated by friendly governments or supportive NGOs from all over the world. The majority of ANC cadres had no access to power and as such could not be corrupt. As a result, the idea of these cadres ever becoming corrupt appeared remote.

Although it is true that in the daily struggle to survive some cadres of the ANC did engage in all manner of criminality, corruption and crime was not the preoccupation of the ANC in exile. Anyone among ANC intellectuals who would have spent time theorising about anti-corruption measures in exile would have been considered weird, or an apartheid spy; cadres would not have understood why valuable time should be devoted to a problem that did not seem real.

Yet the problem of corruption had threatened governments led by revolutionary parties long before the ANC was banned. Upon ascent to power in 1949, Mao Zedong's Communist Party took extraordinary measures to fight corruption among party cadres who now had jobs in the state. The measures included confessions by corrupt cadres, as well as forcing senior bureaucrats, from time to time, to go to work in rural areas in order for them not to lose touch with the people. Some officials were literally killed for being found corrupt.

The Communist Party in Soviet Russia was also not immune from corruption. In fact, the main quarrel that Mao Zedong had with the Soviet communists was that their party was run by a small elite of party cadres who did as they wished, and that bureaucrats were so powerful that they got away with murder.

All this happened before 1960, the year the ANC was banned. Yet the party did not learn lessons; it still did not envisage corruption as a cancer that would attack its own body and that of its government post-apartheid. Worse, the ANC did not even learn from experiences on the African continent, of governments run by liberation parties that went mad. Two decades of an ANC-led government have now revealed that the party was indeed naive. Corruption could be argued to have almost become the party's new emblem.

Like the cadres of Mao Zedong's Communist Party of China, ANC cadres, too, are human beings; they enjoy the good life that comes with the perks of high office. They, too, love to live in mansions, and they also love driving luxury cars. This is what has corrupted the soul of the ANC beyond repair.

When it is profitable to hold public office, and if a party is increasingly perceived as a shortcut to public office, that party will always attract opportunists to its ranks. When this happens factions inevitably form, and the party gets torn apart by members positioning themselves to take over its leadership, and ultimately the state. Once a faction has taken over the state, it uses the state to reward its supporters and punish its detractors.

The factionalisation of party and state is very dangerous in that it erodes public confidence in public institutions. When the public loses confidence in public institutions, institutions suffer a legitimacy crisis. This eventually leads to the collapse of institutions, with dire social implications. When the public becomes aware that public institutions can no longer be trusted as neutral arbiters, citizens retreat either into apathetic individualism or into all-or-nothing interest groups.

Apathetic individualism may seem innocuous among the rich, who have the means to purchase the goods they want from the private sphere, but collectively it leads to the development of a private sub-state, producing and selling the services that ordinarily should be provided by the state. Citizens who live in a private sub-state do not engage in social causes – as long as they can purchase the services they need or desire from private service providers. In the end, however, the growth of a private sub-state is a sign that the state 'proper' is weakening, and this is ultimately not good for society.

Among the poor, apathetic individualism is potentially explosive. When the poor lose confidence in public institutions, they resort to violent means of dispute resolution, such as vigilantism. In a country such as South Africa, where there is a history of violence, it is doubly dangerous for the poor to lose confidence in the state. Whenever there are protests about service delivery, the police battle to maintain order. Sometimes the protests lead to loss of life. A country in which the poor do not believe that the state can or will someday improve their lot is a country without hope. A country where the majority of citizens are poor and without hope is a powder keg waiting to explode. It is worse for South Africa, where the majority of its youth are unemployed, poor and hopeless. This is youthful energy that is boiling; no one knows when it will burst – but burst it will.

The all-or-nothing phenomenon of interest groups is also very dangerous. When public institutions are weak and not trusted by the public, citizens seek protection from interest groups. Interest groups are normal in democracies, but they are strongest where public institutions are weakest. Knowing that public institutions are discredited, individuals strengthen interest groups at the expense of public interests. In fact, interest groups are viewed as embodiments of public interests, even though what is considered public is not what affects the rest of society, but what affects members of this or the other interest group.

When citizens have withdrawn from the real public space, whose strength is in public institutions, the interest groups they rely on tend to be relentless in pursuing their own narrow interests. A prime example of this in latter-day South Africa are leaders and members of the South African Democratic Teachers Union (SADTU). Their demands are paramount. Members of SADTU do not care about the future of the children they are supposed to prioritise. They do as they please, and if this means bringing education to a halt, with no regard for the children of the poor, that, under SADTU, is what will happen.

The general approach in interest-group-driven societies is parleying: what does my side get out of this? The central question is not what it should be, that is, what is good for society? What matters most are what members of interest groups regard as protective of their interests. Ironically, such an environment requires strong public institutions to mediate, but who can mediate between a strong SADTU and a weak and discredited ANC government?

Ultimately, apathetic individualism and an all-or-nothing approach culminate in the withering away of what is truly public, that which cuts across narrow interests – individual interests or those of interest groups. This leaves behind a society without a soul, a society without common values or common public goods. Such a society is characterised by all manner of oddities, such as extreme forms of violence, antisocial behaviour expressed in public, disrespect for public laws and rules and so on.

These things are not rare in post-apartheid South Africa. They are part of our daily reality. They are a sign of a broken society, a society that has been emasculated by the weaknesses of public institutions. It is a society where well-off citizens have withdrawn into an ever-strengthening private sub-state, a society where the poor majority are hopeless and vulnerable to manipulation by all manner of opportunists.

This is the society which has evolved under the leadership of the ANC. What is disheartening is that there is no evidence that the party has what it takes to reverse this frightening trend. Its cadres are too mired in a party life of corruption, factionalism and general decay. For them, chasing material wealth is more of a priority than agonising over the weakening of public institutions. The dictatorship of money has seized complete hold of ANC cadres, and our society is suffering the consequences.

Is society so hapless? So far, yes. As we have suggested in this book, the heroism of the ANC, earned during the liberation struggle, and the magnanimity of Nelson Mandela, demonstrated during the transition years and the period when he served as state president, have created the illusion of a big party which is in control. This has given force to the perception that, outside the party, individuals in society are powerless. The party is regarded as too big to be challenged by ordinary members of society.

Given that South Africa's electoral politics is organised around parties, not individuals, ordinary members of society who are concerned about the worsening state of affairs do not feel emboldened to stand in front of the gigantic wheel of party politics that is rolling and crushing individuals who stand like ants before it. They run for cover in individual cocoons, far away from the bulldozing wheels of party politics.

The only speed humps to disturb the flow of the ANC are a few fragmented opposition parties which in the bigger scheme of things cannot really stop the ANC. A car does not make a U-turn because a road has speed humps; it slows down and resumes high speed as soon as it has gone over the humps. This is exactly what the ANC does: the party forges ahead with what it wants to do regardless of the noise made by opposition parties, for the ANC knows that these parties cannot really stop it at the polls.

Aware that people perceive it as powerful, the ANC continues to do as it pleases, indifferent to any public outcry against corruption and the sapping of the moral content of public institutions. What the party does not seem to realise is that the more it bulldozes the public, the weaker it becomes in the public eye. What the ANC needs to note is that parties first decline in the minds of citizens for some time before the manifestations of public disenchantment are observable practically, through elections and the dwindling of party membership.

If the ANC were to continue bulldozing the public, as we have suggested it will most likely do, society will reach a boiling point and this is when the ANC will fall like a ton of bricks. The fall of the ANC would obviously beg the question: what next? We have suggested several scenarios in this book. It is up to South Africans to begin imagining their possible futures and to ponder the kind of future society they want. In doing so, South Africans must remember:

> Under democracy the differences that matter most are those that lie in the future rather than those we have inherited from the past. Under democracy prophesy speaks louder than memory.[1]

The ANC is aware of this, which is why it keeps on beating the drum of memory, so that our consciousness is locked up perpetually in the prison of history. The objective of this trickery is to have us believe that there is no point in imagining the future, as the future will replay the past. Given that the past is what the ANC claims to have done, the party would like us to believe that the future lies in its glorious past.

Generations of young South Africans who did not witness the past are fed the lie that there was a time in history when the ANC was pure and perfect, and that this purity and perfection will in future be restored.

History is important in so far as it teaches us lessons about our current conditions so that we may avoid previous follies. But history is dangerous when it is used to blunt the blades of imagination. In the end, humanity is caught between two spaces: history and the future. Do we live towards history or the future? By over-blowing the trumpet of history, the ANC wants contemporary South Africans to remain trapped in history. The truth, however, is that no one ever lives in the past. We live today and tomorrow until we die. Those who lived in the past are dead. To be obsessed with the world of the dead, as the ANC would like South Africans to be, is to glorify the grave, as if there is life in the grave. 'Viva the grave!' the ANC wants us to chant.

If South Africans allow the ANC to let memory speak louder than prophecy, they must know that they are robbing themselves of what democracy is all about: the constant contemplation of a better future, not a better past. While we have traced the historical evolution of South Africa in this book, nostalgia is far from our aim. What we have sought to do is make South Africans aware of how the country got where it is, and how to avoid past mistakes, in the effort to build a better country. We trust that this book will be viewed in this light.

ACKNOWLEDGEMENTS

M any discussions in which we took part on the conditions of South African politics and the crisis of leadership in the ANC took place in the scintillating atmosphere of the Midrand Group. This intellectually unique group is an association of young aspirant thinkers who yearn to contribute positively to the building of a better South Africa. It is not possible in our lifetime to repay all that we owe the Midrand Group for its contribution to the way we think.

In its collective outlook, the Midrand Group is generally sceptical of the conventional political parties that have promised heaven on Earth but show little of the leadership capacities or clarity of ideas required to effect meaningful change in society. This critical attitude runs through this book.

Brutus Malada, an exceptionally talented member of the Midrand Group, deserves to be singled out. He read and reread bits, chapters and the whole manuscript before what you are reading resembled a book. Not only did he read; he instructed us to return to the library, to find more evidence to back up some of the wildest claims we had made. What you are reading partly showcases the sharpness of Malada's eye.

Although we have been inspired by the Midrand Group and its ideas, as authors we take full responsibility for the views expressed here. We drew heavily on our own observations and many hours of dialogue about the direction our country is taking and the kind of future our leaders are casting. By this we mean to make it plain that this book is wholly ours.

END NOTES AND REFERENCES

Introduction

1 A detailed analytic examination of liberation movements in power, in particular focusing on southern Africa, can be found in Southall, R. 2013. *Liberation Movements in Power*. Pietermaritzburg: University of KwaZulu-Natal Press.
2 De Tocqueville, A. 1856. *The Old Regime and the French Revolution*. London: Fontana, pp. 33–34.
3 Marcuse, H. 2000. *Reason and Revolution: Hegel and the Rise of Social Theory*. London: Routledge, pp. 10–11.

Chapter 1

1 Keynes, J.M. 2005. *The Economic Consequences of the Peace*. New York: Cosimo, pp. 10–12.
2 Southall, R. 2013. *Liberation Movements in Power: Party and State in Southern Africa*. Pietermaritzburg: University of KwaZulu-Natal Press, p. 18.
3 Hobbes, T. 1985. *Leviathan*. London: Penguin Books, p. 185.
4 Van Riebeeck, J., cited in Feinstein, C.H. 2005. *An Economic History of South Africa: Conquest, Discrimination and Development*. New York: Cambridge University Press, p. 15.
5 Binckes, R. 2013. *The Great Trek Uncut*. Solihull: Helion & Company, p. 38.
6 Meredith, M. 2007. *Diamonds, Gold and War: The Making of South Africa*. Cape Town: Jonathan Ball, p. 2.
7 South African History Online. 'Slavery is Abolished at the Cape'. www.sahistory.org.za/dated-event/slavery-abolished-cape (accessed 3 May 2013).
8 The earlier history of the Afrikaner people and the travails they went through is

extensively discussed in Giliomee, H. 2011. *The Afrikaners: Biography of a People*. London: Hurst and Company.

9   De Kiewiet, C.W. 1957. *A History of South Africa: Social and Economic*. Oxford: Oxford University Press, p. 17.

10   Lentin, A. 2010. *Jan Smuts: Man of Courage and Vision*. Cape Town: Jonathan Ball, p. 27.

11   On the relationship between apartheid and Nazism, see Furlong, P.J. 1991. *Between Crown and Swastika*. Johannesburg: Wits University Press.

12   Meredith, *Diamonds, Gold and War*, pp. 116–117.

13   Meredith, *Diamonds, Gold and War*, p. 200.

14   Mitchell, K. and Mitchell, L. 1910. *The Life and Times of the Right Honourable Cecil John Rhodes 1853–1902*. Charleston: BiblioLife, LLC.

15   Terreblanche, S. 2002. *A History of Inequality in South Africa: 1652–2002*. Pietermaritzburg: University of KwaZulu-Natal Press and Johannesburg: KKM Review Publishing, p. 6.

16   Cited in Giliomee, H. 2012. *The Last Afrikaner Leaders: A Supreme Test of Power*. Cape Town: Tafelberg, p. 30.

17   Giliomee, *The Last Afrikaner Leaders*, p. 13.

18   Posel, D. 2012. 'The Apartheid Project: 1948–1970'. In Mager, A.K., Nasson, B. and Ross, R. (eds) *The Cambridge History of South Africa Volume 2*. Cape Town: Cambridge University Press, p. 321.

19   These words are attributed to Hendrik Verwoerd, then South African Minister for Native Affairs, while reflecting on the education policies of his government during the 1950s. The words have been cited widely by various writers.

20   Seme, P. 'Regeneration of Africa'. Speech delivered at Columbia University. 5 April 1906.

21   Pan Africanist Congress. 'Section 2(c)'. *1959 Constitution*.

22   Biko, S. 2004. *I Write What I Like*. Johannesburg: Picador Africa, p. 77.

Chapter 2

1   African National Congress. 1992. 'Introduction'. In 'Ready to Govern: ANC Policy Guidelines for a Democratic South Africa'.

2   Fukuyama, F. 2011. *The Origins of Political Order: From Prehuman Times to the French Revolution*. London: Profile Books, p. 139.

3   Van Zyl Slabbert, F. 2006. *The Other Side of History: An Anecdotal Reflection on Political Transition in South Africa*. Cape Town: Jonathan Ball, p. 39.

4   Popper, K. 2003. *The Open Society and its Enemies*, Volume One. New York: Routledge Classics, p. 4.

5   See Lenin, V.I. 1917. 'Imperialism, the Highest Stage of Capitalism'. Published as a pamphlet in Petrograd.

6   Marx, K. 1976. *Capital, Volume 1*. London: Penguin Books, p. 929.

7 Marx, *Capital, Volume 1.*

8 Popper, K. 2002. *Conjectures and Refutations: The Growth of Scientific Knowledge.* New York: Routledge, p. 60.

9 African National Congress. 1989. A discussion document on 'Constitutional Guidelines for a Democratic South Africa'.

10 African National Congress 'Consitutional Guidelines'.

11 African National Congress 'Ready to Govern'.

12 Terreblanche, S. 2012. *Lost in Transformation: South Africa's Search for a New Future Since 1986.* Johannesburg: KKM Review Publishing, p. 55.

13 Terreblanche, *Lost in Transformation,* p. 58.

14 Netshitenze, J. 'There is Virtue in Strength and Certainty'. *Sunday Times.* 4 April 2004.

15 News24. 'Zuma's Heaven Remark no Earthly Good'. 7 February 2011. www.news24.com/SouthAfrica/Politics/Zumas-heaven-remark-no-earthly-good-20110207 (accessed 28 May 2013).

16 Esterhuyse, W. 2012. *Endgame: Secret Talks and the End of Apartheid.* Cape Town: Tafelberg, p. 165.

17 *The Economist.* 'Hold your Nose: The Smell of Corruption'. 3 June 2010.

18 Alexander, N. 2002. *An Ordinary Country: Issues in the Transition from Apartheid to Democracy in South Africa.* Pietermaritzburg: University of KwaZulu-Natal Press, p.143.

19 Esterhuyse, *Endgame,* pp. 256–257.

20 The Presidency of the Republic of South Africa. 2008. *Towards a Fifteen Year Review.* p. 19.

Chapter 3

1 Mbeki, T. 1999. 'Democracy is Sure Route to Stability'. *Sunday Independent.* 3 October 1999.

2 Alexander, *An Ordinary Country,* p. 115.

3 Berlin, I., quoted in Hobsbawm, E. 1994. *Age of Extremes: The Short Twentieth Century: 1914–1991.* London: Abacus, p. 5.

4 Lentin, *Jan Smuts,* p. 57.

5 Esterhuyse, *Endgame,* p. 279.

6 Ludi, G. 2011. *The Communistisation of the ANC.* South Africa: Galago Publishing Limited, p. 286.

7 Burns, J.M. 1979. *Leadership.* New York: HarperCollins, p. 20.

8 Sen, A. 1999. *Development as Freedom.* New York: Oxford University Press.

9 Congress of the People. 'Freedom Charter'. Kliptown. 26 June 1955.

10 Kohli, A. 1999. 'Where Do High-Growth Political Economies Come From? The Japanese Lineage of Korea's "Developmental State"'. In Woo-Cumings, M. (ed.). *The Developmental State.* Ithaca: Cornell University Press, p. 93.

11 Johnson, C. 1999. 'The Developmental State: Odyssey of a Concept'. In Woo-Cumings (ed.), *The Developmental State*, p. 53.

12 Cumings, B. 1999. 'Webs with No Spiders, Spiders with No Webs'. In Woo-Cumings (ed.), *The Developmental State*, p. 69.

13 This draws on the Aristotelian critique of the fusion between the state and society, arguing that in an authoritarian setting the state becomes more like a household. Essentially, the state takes on a more paternalistic character. See Aristotle. 1992. *The Politics*. London: Penguin Books.

14 Terreblanche, *Lost in Transformation*, p. 66.

15 Sen, *Development as Freedom*, p. 42.

16 Sen, *Development as Freedom*.

17 African National Congress. 1994. *The Reconstruction and Development Programme*. Johannesburg: Umanyano Publications, pp. 6–7.

18 Nattrass, N. and Seekings, J. 2002. 'Democratic Institutions and Development in Post-Apartheid South Africa'. In Robinson, M. and White, G. (eds). *The Democratic Developmental State: Political and Institutional Design*. Oxford: Oxford University Press, p. 221.

19 A book by Alan Hirsch (2005), an economic adviser in the presidency, concedes that in hindsight there were mistakes in Gear, but makes an apologetic case for the reforms that were undertaken. See Hirsch, A. 2005. *Season of Hope: Economic Reform under Mandela and Mbeki*. Pietermaritzburg: University of KwaZulu-Natal Press.

20 Banerjee, A., Galiani, S., Levinsohn, J., McLaren, Z. and Woolard, I. October 2006. 'Why has Unemployment Risen in the New South Africa?' *Centre for International Development Working Paper*. No. 134. Harvard.

21 Rankin, N., Roberts, G., Schöer, V. and Shepherd, D. 2012. 'The Financial Crisis and its Enduring Legacy for Youth Unemployment'. In Hofmeyr, J. (ed.). *Transformation Audit 2012*. Wynberg: Institute for Justice and Reconciliation.

22 Sharma, R. 2013. *Breakout Nations: In Pursuit of the Next Economic Miracles*. New York: Allen Lane, p. 174.

23 Kierkegaard, S. 1846. *The Crowd is Untruth*. New York: Peter Lang Publishing.

24 Collins, J. 2001. *Good to Great*. London: Random House, p. 85.

25 Hobsbawm, E. 1998. *On History*. New York: New Press, p. 47.

26 Engels, F. and Marx, K. 1970. *The German Ideology*. Edited and with an introduction by Arthur, C.J. London: Lawrence and Wishart.

27 Eagleton, T. 2007. *Ideology: An Introduction*. London: Verso, p. 5.

28 Shubin, V. 2008. *ANC: A View from Moscow*. Auckland Park: Jacana Media, p. 106.

29 Hobsbawm, *On History*, p. 7.

Chapter 4

1 Acemoğlu, D. and Robinson, J. 2012. *Why Nations Fail: The Origins of Power,*

Prosperity and Poverty. New York: Random House.

2 Acemoğlu and Robinson, *Why Nations Fail*.

3 Chabal, P. and Daloz, J. 1999. *Africa Works: Disorder as Political Instrument*. Indiana: Indiana University Press.

4 Gilder, B. 'Tackle all Dimensions of Corruption'. *Sunday Independent*. 12 August 2012.

5 Feinstein, A. 2007. *After the Party*. Cape Town: Jonathan Ball.

6 Adam, H., Moodley, K. and Van Zyl Slabbert, F. 1997. *Comrades in Business: Post-Liberation Politics in South Africa*. Cape Town: Tafelberg, p. 178.

7 Makhura, D. 'Address on the Occasion of the Official Opening of Bheki Mkhize Branch Office'. 20 November 2011.

8 *The Times*. 'Cosatu Appalled at R24.8 Billion Wasted Government Funds'. 20 March 2013. www.timeslive.co.za/local/2013/03/20/cosatu-appalled-at-r24.8-billion-wasted-government-funds (accessed 25 June 2013).

9 Van Zyl Slabbert, *The Other Side of History*, p. 135.

10 Shubin, *ANC*.

11 Ellis, S. 2012. *External Mission: The ANC in Exile, 1960–1990*. Cape Town: Jonathan Ball.

12 Ellis, *External Mission*, pp. 82–83.

13 Esterhuyse, *Endgame*, p. 306.

14 *Mail & Guardian*. 'ANC: Nothing Wrong with Zuma's Call for Support from Business'. 15 January 2013.

15 Hoffman, D.E. 2002. *The Oligarchs: Wealth and Power in New Russia*. New York: Public Affairs.

16 Freeland, C. 2000. *Sale of the Century: The Inside Story of the Second Russian Revolution*. London: Abacus.

17 Russell, A. 2009. *After Mandela: The Battle for the Soul of South Africa*. London: Hutchinson, p. 58.

18 Fukuyama, F. 1995. *Trust: The Social Virtues and the Creation of Prosperity*. New York: Free Press.

19 Popper, *The Open Society*, p. 128.

20 Rotberg, R. 2012. *Transformative Political Leadership*. Chicago: University of Chicago Press.

21 Chabal and Daloz, *Africa Works*, p. 16.

22 Chabal and Daloz, *Africa Works*, p. 16.

Chapter 5

1 Davidson, A. and Filatova, I. 2013. *The Hidden Thread: Russia and South Africa in the Soviet Era*. Cape Town: Jonathan Ball, p. 87.

2 Ludi, *The Communistisation of the ANC*, p. 55.

3 South African Communist Party. 'Section 3.1'. *Constitution*.

4 Lenin, V.I. 1905. 'Two Tactics of Social Democracy in a Democratic Revolution'. In Lenin, V.I. *Collected Works, Volume 9*. pp. 24–25.

5 See Fukuyama, F. 1992. *The End of History and the Last Man*. New York: Free Press.

6 See Joe Slovo's pamphlet. January 1990. 'Has Socialism Failed?'

7 Address by Charles Nqakula to Cosatu Special Congress. Soweto. September 1993.

8 Yeltsin, B. 'Speech to a Meeting of Democratic Russia'. Moscow. 1 June 1991.

9 Althusser, L. 1971. *On Ideology*. London: Verso, p. 67.

10 Lenin, V.I. 1976. *What is to be Done?* London: Penguin, p. 76.

11 Lenin, *What is to be Done?*, p. 76.

12 Gevisser, M. 2007. *Thabo Mbeki: The Dream Deferred*. Cape Town: Jonathan Ball.

13 Kgalema Motlanthe quoted in Adam, Moodley and Van Zyl Slabbert, *Comrades in Business*, p. 3.

14 Thomas, D.P. 2007. 'The South African Communist Party in the Post-Apartheid Period'. In *Review of African Political Economy*. No. 111, pp. 123–138.

15 Oliver Tambo. 'Make South Africa Ungovernable: Broadcast on Radio Freedom'. 10 October 1984.

16 News24. 'Political Hyenas in Feeding Frenzy – Vavi'. 26 August 2012. www.news24.com/news24/SouthAfrica/Politics/Political-hyenas-in-feeding-frenzy-20100826 (accessed 26 August 2013).

Chapter 6

1 Popper, K. 2002. *The Poverty of Historicism*. New York: Routledge, p. 80.

2 This chapter was developed from Prince Mashele's article (2010) 'Losing Contact with the People'. In *The Thinker*. Volume 13, pp. 44–45.

3 Nkrumah, K. 1973. *Revolutionary Path*. London: Panaf Books, p. 13.

4 Wrong, M. 2001. *In the Footsteps of Mr Kurtz: Living on the Brink of Disaster in Mobutu's Congo*. London: Fourth Estate, p. 5.

5 Wa Thiong'o, N. 2006. *Wizard of the Crow*. London: Harvill Secker, pp. 13–15.

6 Mugabe, R. 'Address to the Nation by the Prime Minister Elect'. 4 March 1980.

7 Cabral, A. 1974. *Revolution in Guinea*. London: Stage 1, p. 70.

8 Orwell, G. 2003. *Animal Farm*. London: Penguin Classics, p. 90.

9 Wrong, M. 2009. *It's our Turn to Eat: The Story of a Kenyan Whistleblower*. London: Fourth Estate, p. 61.

Chapter 7

1 Reade, W.W. 2004. *The Martyrdom of Man*. Hawaii: University Press of the Pacific, pp. 274–275.

2 Marcuse, H. 2002. *One-Dimensional Man*. New York: Routledge Classics, p. 69.

3 African National Congress, 'Ready to Govern'.

4 African National Congress, 'Ready to Govern'.

5 Kariem, A. and Mbete, S. 2012. 'Building a Future for South Africa's Youth'. In Hofmeyr, *Transformation Audit 2012*, p. 6.

6 Ferguson, N. 2008. *The Ascent of Money: A Financial History of the World.* New York: Penguin, p. 1.

7 Xiaobo, L. 2000. *Cadres and Corruption: The Organisational Involution of the Chinese Communist Party.* San Francisco: Stanford University Press, pp. 35–36.

Chapter 8

1 Mazibuko, L. 'Campaign Diary Week 5: DA Manifesto Launch Marks Beginning of Election 2011'. Press release. 30 March 2011.

2 Marcuse, *Reason and Revolution*, p. 16.

3 Popper, *The Open Society*, p. 188.

4 Eagleton, T. 2004. *After Theory*. London: Penguin, p. 22.

Chapter 9

1 Bettelheim, B. 1960. 'Foreword'. In Nyiszli, M. *Auschwitz*. New York: Arcade Publishing.

2 Sacks, J. 1997. *The Politics of Hope*. New York: Jonathan Cape.

3 Berlin, I. 1969. *Four Essays on Liberty*. Oxford: Oxford University Press.

4 Chesterton, G.K. 2009. *The Essential GK Chesterton Collection*. Kindle edition via Amazon.com.

Conclusion

1 Unger, R.M. 2005. *What Should the Left Propose?* London: Verso, p. 11.

INDEX